S0-BEC-492

# Financing the Growth of Electric Utilities

# David L. Scott

The Praeger Special Studies program—utilizing the most modern and efficient book production techniques and a selective worldwide distribution network—makes available to the academic, government, and business communities significant, timely research in U.S. and international economic, social, and political development.

# Financing the Growth of Electric Utilities

PRAEGER SPECIAL STUDIES IN INTERNATIONAL BUSINESS, FINANCE, AND TRADE

**Praeger Publishers**  New York  Washington  London

Library of Congress Cataloging in Publication Data

Scott, David Logan, 1942 -
   Financing the growth of electric utilities.

   (Praeger special studies in U.S. economic, social,
and political issues)
   Bibliography: p.
   Includes index
   1. Electric utilities—United States—Costs. I. Title.
HD9685.U5S37          338.4'3          75-25024
ISBN 0-275-56460-6

Robert Manning Strozier Library

JAN 12 1978

Tallahassee, Florida

PRAEGER PUBLISHERS
111 Fourth Avenue, New York, N.Y. 10003, U.S.A.

Published in the United States of America in 1976
by Praeger Publishers, Inc.

*All rights reserved*

© 1976 by Praeger Publishers, Inc.

Printed in the United States of America

To my parents, Robert and Marcia Scott

After decades of declining costs, relative prosperity, and docile consumers, the electric power industry has run into a period of financial uncertainty. The Edison Electric Institute recently reported that by the end of September 1975, investor-owned electric utilities had received approval on 175 requests for increases in rates totaling $2.4 billion. Also pending at that time before regulatory commissions were additional requests for 189 rate increases totaling $4.2 billion.

New rate increases that would raise the average monthly bill for District of Columbia consumers by $4.37 have been recently sought by the Potomac Electric Power Company (PEPCO). This request, which was made in the last days of December 1975, came but six weeks after the Public Service Commission granted the utility a $27.7 million rate increase, thereby raising the basic electric bill of residential customers by $1.82. In Maryland, PEPCO has applied for a $51.8 million rate increase. W. Reid Thompson, the president of PEPCO, explained the need for the increases was tied to the fact that runaway costs were being recorded in every area of the company's operation. He observed that the current financial situation at PEPCO had effectively foreclosed the company from all sources of permanent external financing. Higher rates would, then, allow the company to improve its financial condition sufficiently to permit financing on reasonable terms.

In New York, a request by Consolidated Edison for a 29.3 percent increase in electric rates was reduced by a Public Service Commission examiner to 6.4 percent. The staff of the commission had recommended a 13.6 percent increase. Con Ed company officers also asserted that the company should be allowed to earn 17 percent on its stockholder's investment. The company's current cost of equity investment was reported as between 15 and 16 percent.

A controversial effort by a consortium of electric companies headed by Southern California Edison Company, planning a $3.5 billion Kaiparowits coal-fired power plant in Utah, has been delayed for an indefinite length of time because of pressures from environmental groups and complex regulatory procedures.

One estimate of expenditures by the electric power industry for new facilities during the next 15 years is that they will total $650 billion while external financing will reach $400 billion. The Federal Power Commission's "Financial Outlook for the Electric Power Industry" notes that during the past five years, external financing by the industry increased from 0.5 percent of gross national product to 1 percent, where it is expected to remain, subject to minor decreases from conservation or load leveling.

As Dr. Scott states, the two central problems for the electric utilities to deal with are inflation and fuel prices. Unfortunately, these are variables over which no absolute control may be exerted by the industry. However, there are a number of possibilities which may be considered as opportunities for the electric power industry in an attempt to stabilize itself and thereby hopefully set a standard for revitalization.

The Federal Power Commission allows that the financial condition of the industry will not be strengthened unless the general inflation is brought under control and needed rate increases are granted promptly. The commission also suggests that 1) electric rate increases be held to a minimum consistent with the public's need for energy and economic resource allocation; 2) the rates be raised sufficiently to cover costs and attract the capital needed to finance new electric facilities; 3) the public be made aware of the critical need for adequate rates; 4) rate structures be modified to encourage conservation of capital as well as energy—this being accomplished by modifying rate structures so as to trim peak loads and shift use to nighttime, weekend, and seasonal valleys; 5) regulatory processes be streamlined in order to deal with inflation; 6) tax policies be designed to stimulate and reward individual savings and investment—possibly by allowing tax-free reinvestment of dividends in new-issue stock; 7) discriminatory tax policies reflect both costs and benefits; and, finally, 8) the capital needs of public-owned systems be recognized and their financial integrity not eroded by budget or financing restrictions, nor their ability to participate in joint ventures unreasonably impeded.

In its report, "Electricity and the Environment," the Association of the Bar of the City of New York's Special Committee on Electric Power and the Environment stated three ways more efficient production on energy use could be obtained; government rationing of energy or energy-using equipment such as appliances; government action directed toward internalizing the external costs of energy use—not abated by direct regulation—by taxing energy or its pollutants; and government action aimed at requiring that buildings and equipment be designed to minimize energy use. These actions were regarded as not mutually exclusive. The obvious weakness of these proposals, however, is that they are designed to substitute governmental decisions for private decisions normally made by individuals and firms. But there is another reason why—if implemented—these actions would only go, in a limited way, to resolve problems. These suggestions, while perfectly rational, fail to come to grips with the root cause of the total problem of the electric utility industry. For it is in the financing of the electric power industry that the primary cause of the problem and its potential resolution is to be found.

During the closing days of 1975, President Gerald R. Ford's Administration acknowledged its efforts to convince the Saudi Arabian government to invest upwards to $1 billion in the "cash-starved" United States electric utilities. The Saudis indicated they would be interested in investing undetermined amounts in individual electric companies of their own choosing. The money—when and if forthcoming—would initially be in the form of loans.

Dr. Scott far exceeds his stated purpose of affording the reader with an overall view of the electric power industry as well as a detailed investigation of its financial mechanisms. He has, rather, submitted a solid blueprint for resolving a vexatious environmental and financial conundrum. More specifically, he proposes an elimination of the fuel adjustment charge; avoidance of subsidies to the industry such as a federal guarantee on debt; tariff schedules be flattened in combination with an increased usage of peak-load pricing; an increase in the allowed rate of return and a minimization of regulatory lag and inclusion of construction work-in-progress within the rate base.

This seminal investigation presented by Dr. Scott bears careful and thoughtful consideration.

# PREFACE

The electric utility industry has attracted increasing public attention, ranging across a broad spectrum from genuine concern to outright hostility. The two primary areas of concern have centered on the financial health of the industry and the related problem of its ability to provide adequate capacity to meet future power requirements. General unhappiness by the public was first evident during the 1960s via demands for an environmental cleanup, but rapidly switched to outcries over higher utility rates subsequent to the Arab oil embargo. While nearly all people familiar with the industry's problems agree that higher rates are necessary and continue to be of primary importance, there is less accord on exactly how the rate increases should be structured. An increasing number of individuals are calling for a revamping of the traditional declining block-rate structures. It is argued that at a time when the electric utilities are striving to raise additional billions of dollars to meet inflation-bloated construction requirements, the typical rate structures continue to penalize smaller users. Regardless of how the new expenditures are financed or what rate structures are finally implemented, however, the trend to higher rates is inevitable.

Appreciation is given to *Electrical World* and its editor, William C. Hayes, for allowing me to use data from that publication's Annual Electrical Industry Forecasts. I would also like to thank the Research Fund Advisory Committee at Valdosta State College for its financial support of this project. I express gratitude to Gloria Parker, Connie Murphy, Janie Dacus, and Lynn Carroll for help in typing the manuscript, and to Virginia Carmona, Walter Turner, and Bill Fredenberger for helping to read and research early drafts. I am particularly indebted to Marvin Ray, my good friend and colleague at VSC, for his detailed review of the entire manuscript. Finally I am grateful to my wife, Kay, who puts up with all this.

# CONTENTS

# LIST OF TABLES

# LIST OF FIGURES

# Financing the Growth of Electric Utilities

After years of declining costs and relatively good service, Americans had begun taking the electric power industry for granted. Even scattered blackouts and brownouts due to power outages and overloads were taken by most individuals as little more than nuisances. Very few people outside the industry worried about where new capacity and fuel would come from; most just assumed it would be available when needed—most probably at a price equal to or lower than that currently prevailing. While most citizens, if they thought about it at all, realized that fossil-fuel supplies would eventually become depleted, they assumed that alternative power sources, probably nuclear, would be available when needed.

Financially, the utilities looked strong. The safety of electric utility debt was considered second only to that on U.S. government obligations, and the common stocks of nearly all companies in the industry had shown amazingly consistent growth in both earnings and dividends. Even though most utilities had been adding great amounts of debt to their capital structures in order to finance new plant and equipment, this was thought to be good business practice since interest expense could be used as a deduction against income for tax purposes. While interest coverage ratios were declining due to both higher interest rates and more debt, constantly expanding revenues and cash flow streams could be counted on to more than cover increased fixed expenses. In any case, if for some reason debt became too burdensome, common stock could always be sold at well over book value. The job of a public utility commissioner looked like a plum indeed. One measure of the general lack of concern with the industry was the ebbing interest of both students and faculty members in public utilities courses in colleges and universities throughout the country.

During the latter half of the 1960s, two fundamental changes began to occur which were to shape the industry's future. The first was the gathering

1

steam of inflation and the resulting increase in the cost of debt and equity. The second was the increasing environmental awareness of the public that electric utilities were not paying the full cost of producing their product.

In 1965, inflation began accelerating. With it came higher long-term interest rates, lower price-earnings ratios on common stock, and rising costs for capital equipment. Depreciation and retained earnings proved to be increasingly inadequate in providing funds for inflated capital expenditures; thus, utilities were required to enter the capital markets regardless of the cost of external funds. On top of this came public outcries for the utilities to begin a massive environmental cleanup campaign. In a short period of time, this resulted in federal and state legislation which required the industry to begin spending billions of dollars on pollution abatement equipment.[1]

In response to environmental standards, cost considerations, and problems with nuclear facilities, electric utilities began to put increasing emphasis on oil-fired steam-electric plants. This included the conversion of already existing facilities as well as the planning of new plants which would come on-line at a future date. After the industry had committed itself to increasing the proportion of electric power plants fueled by this primary energy source (between 1968 and 1973 the contribution of this segment increased from 7.8 percent to 16.8 percent of total output),[2] the Arab oil embargo struck. The aftermath of this occurrence is familiar to all. Once the embargo was lifted, oil prices soared and fuel adjustment charges played havoc with the electric bills of both households and businesses. In addition, for political reasons, the federal government shifted toward a policy of having the utilities make greater use of coal resources which were abundantly available in the United States.

Hence, during the last decade, the electric utilities have been buffeted by a number of changes which were not of their own making. Their reaction (or sometimes, lack of reaction) to these changes brought criticism from most of the public, many businessmen, and nearly all legislators. While a relatively small proportion of critics was unsatisfied with the quality of service provided by individual companies, and a larger number found fault in the speed with which utilities were installing pollution abatement and safety equipment, the vast majority of outcries were in reaction to a sharp escalation in the price of electricity. People were suddenly finding that electric bills were occupying a much larger portion of their budgets. When this was combined with the above average price increases for other essential goods and services, such as food, the situation became especially severe. In large part, the higher electric bills represented increased fuel costs to the utilities which were being automatically passed through via fuel adjustment charges to consumers. Rate increases to cover other escalating operating expenses and higher capital costs were being delayed, rejected, or cut back by regulatory commissions which were deluged by complaints from the public over increases in electric bills which had already taken place. Hence, although the industry was generating sufficient funds to pay the higher fuel costs, it was having a much more difficult time in obtaining revenue increases to cover other increased costs, thereby penalizing profits and making it difficult, if not impossible, to sell securities and provide for expansion. Had higher fuel costs not already alienated the public, regulatory commissions quite probably would have been much more generous in allowing other needed rate increases.

While the reduction in demand for electricity which accompanied the higher prices left the utilities with short-term excess capacity problems, it also gave them breathing room in financing new construction expenditures. Due to the difficulty, and in some cases, impossibility, of raising capital funds, many projects were delayed, reduced in scope, or simply canceled. The possibility of making the industry vigorous again is still in question.

A number of good studies on the electric power industry are available. While somewhat dated, the Federal Power Commission's *1970 National Power Survey* is an excellent source of background information on the industry. The commission is now making the *Survey* an ongoing study and a number of committee reports have been completed. One of these, *Task Force Report: Environmental Research*, is available to the general public through the U.S. Government Printing Office.[3] A number of others, however, are in limited distribution. Of particular interest are the FPC Office of Economics' *Analysis of the Electric Utility Industry's Financial Requirements: 1975-79*, which was issued during September of 1974, and the preliminary draft of the *Report of the National Power Survey Technical Advisory Committee on Finance* which was distributed during October of 1974. Both of these reports include estimates of the industry's financial requirements and proposals for improving its capacity for obtaining the necessary funding.

Various congressional hearings have concentrated on the electric utility industry, although many only indirectly apply to financial aspects. Among the better of these are *Hearings on Environmental Effects of Producing Electric Power* before the Joint Committee on Atomic Energy in 1969,[4] *Hearings on Power Plant Siting and Environmental Projection* before the House Subcommittee on Communications and Power in 1971,[5] *Hearings on Problems of Electrical Production in the Southwest* before the Senate Committee on Interior and Insular Affairs in 1971,[6] and hearings by the Subcommittee of the Senate Committee on Commerce concerning energy and environmental objectives.[7] Other studies involved with the industry's cost of environmental protection include *Pollution in the Electric Power Industry,*[8] *Energy and the Environment,*[9] and *The Environmental Crisis and Corporate Debt Capacity.*[10]

Additional congressional hearings which provide good background information on electric utilities are *Hearings on Project Independence* before the Senate Committee on Interior and Insular Affairs in 1974,[11] *Hearings to Create a National Commission on Regulatory Reform* before the Senate Committee on Commerce in 1973,[12] and *Hearings on Conservation and Efficient Use of Energy* before the House Subcommittees of the Committees on Government Operations and Science Astronautics in 1973.[13] A large amount of information on technology, research, and availability of fuels was compiled by the Senate Committee on Interior and Insular Affairs during the National Fuels and Energy Policy Study. A background document for the study, *Electric Utility Policy Issues*,[14] is especially good.

The Energy Policy Project of the Ford Foundation produced over 20 major studies, all of which in one way or another are applicable to electric power. Of special significance to the financing of electric utilities are *Perspective on Power: The Regulation and Pricing of Electricity, Financing the Energy Industry*, and *Studies in Electric Utility Regulation*. The policy project's final report, *A Time to Choose: America's Energy Future*,[15] summarizes all of the studies.

Other studies incorporating financial aspects of electric utilities are *Power Plant Capital Costs: Current Trends and Sensitivity to Economic Parameters*,[16] *The Economic and Environmental Benefits from Improving Electrical Rate Structures*,[17] and Weidenbaum's well-known report for the Edison Electric Institute, *Financing the Electric Utility Industry*.[18]

This study has been designed to include sufficient material to give the reader an overall view of the electric power industry as well as to provide him with a more detailed investigation of its financial mechanisms. Chapter 2 presents a general overview of the industry, including its structure, regulation, and methods of power production. Costs of generation and the pricing of electricity are discussed in Chapter 3, while Chapter 4 reviews traditional methods of financing used by the industry. Chapter 5 projects sources of funds during the period 1976-90, assuming historical trends of financing are employed. A summary, conclusions, and recommendations are presented in Chapter 6.

## NOTES

1. See David L. Scott, *Pollution in the Electric Power Industry: Its Control and Costs* (Lexington, Massachusetts: D. C. Heath and Co., 1973).

2. U.S. Federal Power Commission, *Statistics of Privately Owned Electric Utilities in the United States* (Washington: U.S. Government Printing Office, various years).

3. ———, *Task Force Report: Environmental Research* (Washington: U.S. Government Printing Office, 1974).

4. U.S. Congress, Joint Committee on Atomic Energy, *Hearings on Environmental Effects of Producing Electric Power*, 91st Cong., 2nd Sess., 1969-70.

5. U.S. Congress, House, Subcommittee on Communications and Power, *Hearings on Power Plant Siting and Environmental Protection*, 92nd Cong., 1st Sess., 1971.

6. U.S. Congress, Senate, Committee on Interior and Insular Affairs, *Hearings on Problems of Electrical Production in the Southwest*, 92nd Cong., 1st Sess., 1971.

7. U.S. Congress, Senate, Subcommittee of the Committee on Commerce, *Hearings on Energy and Environmental Objectives*, 93rd Cong., 2nd Sess., 1974.

8. Scott, op. cit.

9. U.S. Council on Environmental Quality, *Energy and the Environment* (Washington: U.S. Government Printing Office, 1973).

10. Marvin E. Ray, *The Environmental Crisis and Corporate Debt Capacity* (Lexington, Massachusetts: D. C. Heath and Co., 1974).

11. U.S. Congress, Senate, Committee on Interior and Insular Affairs, *Hearings on Project Independence*, 93rd Cong., 2nd Sess., 1974.

12. U.S. Congress, Senate, Committee on Commerce, *Hearings to Create a National Commission on Regulatory Reform*, 93rd Cong., 2nd Sess., 1974.

13. U.S. Congress, House, Subcommittees of the Committee on Government Operations and Science and Astronautics, *Hearings on Conservation and Efficient Use of Energy*, 93rd Cong., 1st Sess., 1973.

14. U.S. Congress, Senate, Committee on Interior and Insular Affairs, *Electric Utility Policy Issues* (Washington: U.S. Government Printing Office, 1974).

15. The Ford Foundation Energy Policy Project studies are available from Ballinger Publishing Company.

16. U.S. Atomic Energy Commission, Division of Reactor Research and Development, *Power Plant Capital Costs: Current Trends and Sensitivity to Economic Parameters* (Washington: U.S. Government Printing Office, 1974).

17. U.S. Environmental Protection Agency, Office of Research and Development, *The Economic and Environmental Benefits from Improving Electrical Rate Structures* (Washington: U.S. Government Printing Office, 1974).

18. Murray L. Weidenbaum, *Financing the Electric Utility Industry* (New York: Edison Electric Institute, 1974).

# 2

The electric power industry has traveled a considerable distance from its humble beginnings with Thomas Edison's incandescent bulb and the initial central power generating stations which ensued shortly thereafter. These coal-burning direct-current units operated at low voltages and supplied electricity to nearby consumers primarily for lighting and running motors. As geographical service areas expanded as a result of technological improvements and the accompanying economies of scale, small power companies merged giving rise to reduced competition and a need for increased government attention. Early rule making occurred primarily at the state and local level; however, as holding companies began to dominate a major portion of the operating companies' generating capacity, a need for more comprehensive regulation arose. The initial federal attempt at providing leadership culminated in passage of the Public Utility Act of 1935. This legislation made provisions for more standardized financial and accounting practices, interconnections, and the regulation of interstate wholesale electric rates. However, it dismissed most intrastate matters and left them under control of the states.

## ENERGY AND ELECTRICITY

While the use of electric power expanded greatly during the early 1900s, its continued growth subsequent to the Great Depression was even more startling. From slightly over 91 billion kilowatt hours in 1930, electric generation from central power stations had increased to 1,850 billion kilowatt hours by 1973.[1] This growth was, in turn, a symptom of America's seemingly unquenchable thirst for energy in general. During the same 1930-73 period, the consumption of primary energy increased from 22 trillion Btu (British thermal units) to slightly less than 75 trillion Btu. More recent figures show a similar if less pronounced trend. Since 1955, energy usage has nearly doubled while consumption of electricity has more than tripled. Because the numbers discussed in total energy and electric consumption are somewhat mind boggling, it is helpful to refer to the data on a per capita basis. From 1930 through 1973, the consumption of basic energy per capita in the United States doubled from 181 million to 360 million Btu, while the per capita generation of electricity increased 12 times from 740 to 8,809 kilowatt hours. Since 1955, these increases have been 50 percent and 163 percent, respectively. (Consumption of energy and electricity on both an aggregate and a per capita basis is found in Table 2.1.)

The more rapid growth in the consumption of electricity as compared to primary energy sources (only hydroelectric and nuclear plants generate primary energy) demonstrates a clear preference, and in some cases a necessity, for consumers to use the former power mode. In many cases the transformation or primary energy is necessitated due to the nature of its end use, as for example with electronic equipment. In numerous instances, however, consumers have simply opted for electricity because of its convenient nature.[2] For example, illumination and heating can each be accomplished by using primary energy sources or by conversion of these sources into electrical energy. Electricity's increasing share of the energy market is projected by most experts to continue with the result that electric generating plants will find it necessary to consume an ever larger share of the world's primary energy resources (see Figure 2.1). While a large portion of the increased penetration will be provided by new nuclear power plants, the remaining share must come from fossil fuels until new energy technologies are perfected and come on-line.

As the electric utilities matured toward their present state, the composition of end users began shifting. In the early 1900s, the chief consumer of electrical energy was the industrial sector, and until the end of World War II, industrial users consumed over twice as much electricity as the residential and commercial sectors combined. Following the war, as economic conditions improved and real personal incomes rose, residential demand for electricity skyrocketed. While total sales in terms of kilowatt hours increased by less than 400 percent from 1950 through 1972, residential sales jumped by nearly 650 percent (see Table 2.2). Along with substituting electrical energy for primary energy in some uses, individuals seemed to find a multitude of new products which were powered by only the former. Commercial sales expanded by slightly less than residential sales, increasing approximately 600 percent over the 1950-72 period. The remaining sector, industrial consumption, increased by only 230 percent and had declined to approximately 41 percent of total usage by 1972.

## TABLE 2.1

### Energy Consumption and Electrical Generation in the United States, 1930-73

| Year | Energy | | Electricity | |
|---|---|---|---|---|
| | Total Consumed (billions of Btu) | Per Capita (millions of Btu) | Total Generated (billions of kilowatt hours) | Per Capita (kilowatt hours) |
| 1930 | 22,288 | 181 | 91 | 740 |
| 1935 | 19,107 | 150 | 95 | 748 |
| 1940 | 23,908 | 181 | 141 | 1,068 |
| 1945 | 31,541 | 238 | 222 | 1,675 |
| 1950 | 34,153 | 226 | 328 | 2,161 |
| 1955 | 39,956 | 243 | 547 | 3,297 |
| 1960 | 44,816 | 249 | 754 | 4,169 |
| 1965 | 53,969 | 278 | 1,055 | 5,433 |
| 1966 | 56,412 | 288 | 1,144 | 5,824 |
| 1967 | 58,265 | 294 | 1,212 | 6,115 |
| 1968 | 61,763 | 309 | 1,329 | 6,627 |
| 1969 | 64,979 | 323 | 1,442 | 7,118 |
| 1970 | 67,444 | 332 | 1,531 | 7,469 |
| 1971 | 69,010 | 335 | 1,614 | 7,800 |
| 1972 | 72,108 | 346 | 1,748 | 8,394 |
| 1973 | 75,561 | 360 | 1,850 | 8,809 |

*Sources*: Walter G. Dupree and James A. West, *United States Energy Through the Year 2000* (Washington: U.S. Government Printing Office, 1972); and U.S. Federal Power Commission, *Statistics of Privately Owned Electric Utilities in the United States* (Washington: U.S. Government Printing Office, various years).

## TABLE 2.2

### Sale of Electrical Energy to End Users, 1930-72
#### (billions of kilowatt hours)

| Year | Residential | | Commercial | | Industrial | |
|---|---|---|---|---|---|---|
| | Amount | Percent | Amount | Percent | Amount | Percent |
| 1930 | 11 | 12.8 | 14 | 16.3 | 61 | 70.9 |
| 1935 | 14 | 15.4 | 14 | 15.4 | 63 | 69.2 |
| 1940 | 24 | 17.4 | 22 | 15.9 | 92 | 66.7 |
| 1945 | 38 | 17.9 | 28 | 13.2 | 146 | 68.9 |
| 1950 | 72 | 22.6 | 52 | 16.3 | 195 | 61.1 |
| 1955 | 128 | 24.5 | 79 | 15.1 | 315 | 60.3 |
| 1960 | 201 | 30.7 | 133 | 20.3 | 321 | 49.0 |
| 1965 | 292 | 31.6 | 201 | 21.7 | 432 | 46.7 |
| 1966 | 317 | 31.7 | 218 | 21.8 | 465 | 46.5 |
| 1967 | 340 | 32.1 | 233 | 22.0 | 486 | 45.9 |
| 1968 | 380 | 32.9 | 257 | 22.2 | 519 | 44.9 |
| 1969 | 426 | 35.4 | 281 | 23.3 | 560 | 46.5 |
| 1970 | 467 | 34.7 | 307 | 22.8 | 572 | 42.5 |
| 1971 | 500 | 35.2 | 329 | 23.2 | 590 | 41.6 |
| 1972 | 538 | 35.1 | 359 | 23.4 | 636 | 41.5 |

*Sources:* U.S. Department of Commerce, Bureau of the Census, *Historical Statistics of the United States: Colonial Times to 1957,* Series S 81-93 (Washington: U.S. Government Printing Office), p. 511; and idem, *Statistical Abstract of the United States, 1973* (Washington: U.S. Government Printing Office), p. 509.

## FIGURE 2.1

### U.S. Energy Consumption by Sector,
### 1971-2000
### (quadrillion Btu's)

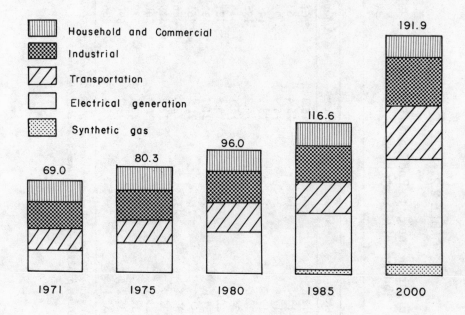

*Source*: Walter G. Dupree and James A. West, *United States Energy Through the Year 2000* (Washington: U.S. Government Printing Office, 1972), reprinted in U.S. Congress, House, Committee on Science and Astronautics, *Energy Facts*, 93rd Cong., 2nd Sess., 1973, p. 49.

## STRUCTURE OF THE INDUSTRY

Four distinct ownership segments comprise the electric utility industry in the United States. These include private corporations owned by investors, public systems of the federal government, electric cooperatives, and nonfederal public systems of states, municipalities, or utility districts. While the latter three types of ownership groups account for the largest number of systems (approximately 2,900 as against nearly 500 private utilities),[3] many of these are relatively small and it is left to the investor-owned utilities to generate and sell the major portion of electrical energy in the United States. A large number of cooperative and nonfederal systems are involved in distribution only and purchase energy from private and federal electric utilities for resale to consumers.

As shown in Table 2.3, installed generating capacity of investor-owned systems accounted for approximately 80 percent of the industry total in 1973. This was an increase from 70 percent in 1960, and nearly the same as the composition which existed in 1950. Following 1950, cooperative systems showed the greatest relative increase in capacity; however, the aggregate generating capacity of all cooperatives in 1973 was still less than half of that which existed for investor-owned systems in 1950. Municipal utilities displayed the most moderate increases in generating capacity subsequent to 1950, rising from 5 million kilowatts to 25 million kilowatts by 1973.

## TABLE 2.3

### Installed Generating Capacity by Type of System, 1930-73 (millions of kilowatts)

| Year | Investor-owned | Municipal | Federal | Cooperative |
|------|----------------|-----------|---------|-------------|
| 1930 | 30 | 2 | * | * |
| 1935 | 32 | 2 | * | * |
| 1940 | 34 | 3 | 2 | * |
| 1945 | 40 | 4 | 5 | 1 |
| 1950 | 55 | 5 | 7 | 2 |
| 1955 | 87 | 8 | 17 | 3 |
| 1960 | 128 | 11 | 22 | 6 |
| 1965 | 178 | 15 | 32 | 11 |
| 1966 | 186 | 17 | 33 | 13 |
| 1967 | 202 | 17 | 34 | 14 |
| 1968 | 221 | 19 | 35 | 16 |
| 1969 | 240 | 20 | 36 | 17 |
| 1970 | 263 | 21 | 39 | 19 |
| 1971 | 287 | 22 | 40 | 19 |
| 1972 | 315 | 23 | 41 | 21 |
| 1973 | 345 | 25 | 44 | 24 |

*Less than 500,000 kilowatts.

Sources: U.S. Department of Commerce, Bureau of the Census, *Historical Statistics of the United States: Colonial Times to 1975*, Series S 61-19 (Washington: U.S. Government Printing Office), p. 509; and idem, *Statistical Abstract of the United States, 1973* (Washington: U.S. Government Printing Office), p. 509.

In terms of generation of electricity, investor-owned utilities accounted for slightly less than 78 percent of the total in 1973 (see Table 2.4). This was up very slightly from 77 percent in 1960 and down somewhat from 81 percent in 1950. Of the remaining three types of utility structures, federal systems consistently generated the most electrical power and supplied 211 million kilowatt hours, or slightly more than 11 percent of total generation in 1973. This was a decline in relative importance from both 1950 and 1960, when this segment of the electric utility industry supplied 12 percent and 15 percent, respectively. The greatest relative increase in generation, as with generating capacity, was by cooperative systems. This component of the industry jumped from 2 percent and 3 percent of total kilowatt hours in 1950 and 1960, respectively, to over 6 percent in 1973.

## TABLE 2.4

### Generation of Electricity by Type of System, 1930-73
### (millions of kilowatt hours)

| Year | Investor-Owned | Municipal | Federal | Cooperative |
|------|----------------|-----------|---------|-------------|
| 1930 | 86    | 4  | *   | 1   |
| 1935 | 89    | 4  | 1   | 1   |
| 1940 | 125   | 6  | 9   | 1   |
| 1945 | 181   | 10 | 28  | 3   |
| 1950 | 267   | 15 | 40  | 6   |
| 1955 | 421   | 26 | 89  | 11  |
| 1960 | 579   | 37 | 112 | 26  |
| 1965 | 809   | 50 | 145 | 51  |
| 1966 | 881   | 53 | 153 | 57  |
| 1967 | 928   | 58 | 162 | 64  |
| 1968 | 1,019 | 64 | 171 | 75  |
| 1969 | 1,102 | 70 | 183 | 87  |
| 1970 | 1,183 | 71 | 186 | 91  |
| 1971 | 1,250 | 73 | 194 | 97  |
| 1972 | 1,357 | 79 | 207 | 105 |
| 1973 | 1,445 | 79 | 211 | 115 |

*Less than 500 million kilowatt hours.

Sources: U.S. Department of Commerce, Bureau of the Census, Historical Statistics of the United States: Colonial Times to 1957, Series S 27-35 (Washington: U.S. Government Printing Office), p. 507; and idem, Statistical Abstract of the United States, 1973 (Washington: U.S. Government Printing Office), p. 509.

As the data in Tables 2.3 and 2.4 make clear, the structure of the electric utilities is in a constant state of flux. During any short-run period, one segment of the industry may be increasing in scope at the expense of one or more of the other groups. In the following period, however, the trend might very well be reversing itself with some new group playing a more important role.

## Investor-Owned Utilities

Investor-owned electric systems, while small in number, dominate the industry in nearly every other respect. They serve more customers, sell more power, consume more fuel, and employ more people than all other segments of the industry combined.

The few hundred private systems which currently exist are an assimilation of over 1,400 companies which prevailed in the latter 1930s and over 2,000 systems which were in existence in the latter 1920s.[4] The private systems which have survived the consolidations of earlier years vary in size from giant integrated corporations to very small independent companies. The largest systems provide nearly all of this segment's generating capacity (the largest two-thirds of investor-owned companies have nearly 78 percent of installed capacity in the United States)[5] while smaller companies generally resell power purchased from other utilities. The immense size of the largest investor-owned systems is more clearly seen by referring to Table 2.5. As a point of reference, Consolidated

## TABLE 2.5

### Ten Largest Investor-Owned Electric Systems, 1973
### (millions of dollars)

| System | Assets[a] | Operating Revenues[b] |
|---|---|---|
| Consolidated Edison | 5,968 | 1,736 |
| Pacific Gas & Electric | 5,471 | 1,490 |
| Southern Company | 5,378 | 1,166 |
| American Electric Power | 5,071 | 966 |
| Commonwealth Edison | 4,469 | 1,266 |
| Southern California Edison | 3,990 | 1,079 |
| Public Service Electric & Gas | 3,897 | 1,076 |
| Philadelphia Electric | 3,176 | 767 |
| Detroit Edison | 3,061 | 753 |
| General Public Utilities | 3,034 | 662 |

[a]Assets are net of depreciation and include consolidated subsidiaries.
[b]Includes nonutility revenues.
Source: Fortune 90, no. 1 (July 1974): 124.

Edison, the largest privately owned electric utility, has more net assets than all but the largest 17 industrial corporations in the United States.[6] This is expecially noteworthy since Consolidated Edison operates in such a comparatively small geographical area. Unfortunately, revenues and profits do not rate nearly so high in a similar comparison.

State and local government agencies or commissions generally grant territorial franchises which can be served by investor-owned systems. The purpose of this certification is to avoid duplication of the heavy fixed expenses which would be required of any effort to promote competition between systems. In some cases a second utility might be permitted to serve a specific territory but the additional company would first be required to exhibit that the addition would serve the public interest.

## Public Nonfederal Utilities

Of the approximately 2,000 electric systems in this segment of the industry, well over half purchase all of their power requirements externally. As such, public nonfederal electric systems generate significantly less electricity than they sell. In recent years, sales have held relatively steady at 150 percent of kilowatt hours generated.

A large majority of the systems which purchase energy for resale serve primarily small communities, while those servicing large metropolitan districts usually generate most or all of their own electrical needs. Examples of systems in this latter category are the Electric Authority of Jacksonville (Florida), the City of Seattle Department of Lighting, and the Department of Water and Power of the City of Los Angeles. These large complexes market power to approximately 175,000, 260,000, and 1,100,000 customers, respectively, and had combined electrical sales in 1971 of over 26 billion kilowatt hours.[7]

While most public nonfederal systems are run by municipalities, there also exist a number of systems run by public utility districts, irrigation districts, and special state authorities. An example of the latter type of unit is the Arizona Power Authority which purchases power from the Bureau of Reclamation and other generating agencies and distributes this through transmission facilities owned by the Bureau of Reclamation.[8] Except for metering equipment, the Arizona system does not own any generation, transmission, or distribution facilities; yet in 1971, it sold nearly 800 million kilowatt hours of electric power.[9] The Power Authority of the State of New York is a similar type of system. In 1971, while it sold electricity to only 56 customers, it made sales of nearly $100 billion, representing over 21 billion kilowatt hours of electrical power.[10]

Public systems outside the federal domain are generally not subject to state and local taxes and are also exempt from federal income taxes. In place of local taxation, however, many systems may make voluntary contributions to municipalities, including free or reduced-rate power.

## Federal Utilities

Electric power generated from federal installations in the United States is marketed through six federal agencies: Bonneville Power Administration, Southeastern Power Administration, Southwestern Power Administration, Alaska Power Administration, the Bureau of Reclamation, and the Tennessee Valley Authority. These six systems are a very significant element in the nation's electric power industry. In 1973, installed generating capacity and generation of electricity by federal utilities equaled 10.1 percent and 11.4 percent, respectively, of all systems.[11] These proportions, while significantly less than the relative contribution of investor-owned companies, were greater than those of either cooperative or public nonfederal systems.

Aside from the Tennessee Valley Authority (TVA), power distributed by federal systems is drawn from hydroelectric projects which serve multipurpose objectives. In addition to electric production, these facilities are designed for navigation, irrigation, and flood control. While the additional activities generally provide little or no revenues, they do play an important part in cost allocation. Costs are assigned to the various uses of a project after a determination has been made of how benefits are to be allocated. For example, depreciation and administration expenses are spread over various uses of a project on the basis of benefits that are perceived to exist in each of the project's functions.[12] Electric rates are therefore determined by the part of total costs assigned to power production plus expenses relating only to electric generation.

All federal systems, including TVA, are required to give preference in the sale of output to cooperatives and public bodies.[13] This output originates from over 125 facilities, most of which are operated under the auspices of the Tennessee Valley Authority, the Bureau of Reclamation, and the Corps of Engineers. The agencies of the Department of the Interior then market all power with the exception of that which is generated at TVA facilities. The greatest part of this electricity is integrated into other electric systems as supplemental energy and sold at wholesale rates; however, a portion is consumed by large industrial users and by federal complexes. Most of the power produced for the latter uses has been designed for base loads and exists primarily in the Northwest and those areas serviced by TVA.[14]

The Pacific Northwest is served by the Bonneville Power Administration through over 30 hydroelectric facilities operated by the Corps of Engineers and the Bureau of Reclamation. Areas in the Far West, the Colorado Basin, the Missouri Basin, and the Southwest are serviced from electric power systems of the Bureau of Reclamation. The Southeastern Power Administration markets energy from hydroelectric projects of the Corps in the South Central states. The Alaska Power Administration markets electric energy from hydroelectric facilities in the state of Alaska. Approximately one-half of the power is distributed to Anchorage with the rest going to cooperatives.

The Tennessee Valley Authority is considerably different than the five power agencies operated under the Department of the Interior. TVA is the nation's largest electric power producer, supplying energy over an area of approximately 80,000 square miles to portions of Tennessee, Alabama, Kentucky, Mississippi, Georgia, Virginia, and North Carolina. It generates, transmits, and distributes electricity to 160 distributors, 48 industries, and 11 federal installations. Sales to cooperative and municipal systems are made at wholesale rates and account for nearly half of aggregate output.

The TVA was originally established in 1933 to develop resources of the Tennessee River Basin, including hydroelectric facilities in conjunction with flood control and navigation. However, it currently produces approximately 78 percent of its energy requirements through a system of 12 coal-fired steam plants. This is significantly above the national average in which 46 percent of the total energy inputs for electric power generation is supplied by coal. Although 13 nuclear plants are scheduled for completion by 1982, thereby reducing the percentage of electricity generated with coal, the consumption of this fossil fuel by TVA plants is expected to increase by 25 percent before 1980.[15]

## Cooperative Utilities

From the time of the first central generating station until 1935, less than 11 percent of farms in the United States had obtained electric energy. In addition to a higher cost of electricity than that which was available in the cities, farmers typically had to pay from $2,000 to $3,000 per mile for construction of lines to their homes.[16] In an effort to stimulate the expansion of electric service into these rural areas, the Rural Electrification Administration (REA) was created in 1935 as a part of unemployment relief under authority of the Emergency Relief Appropriation Act. The initial appropriation was $100 million for loans and grants, although the first year of operation brought little interest from those institutions expected to make applications for investment money. In 1936 additional legislation was introduced in Congress which stipulated that "States, Territories, and Subdivisions and Agencies thereof, municipalities, people's utility districts, and cooperative, non-profit, or limited-dividend associations" be given preference in making REA loans.[17] The Rural Electrification Act of 1936 has been the basis upon which the REA has since operated.

From 29 borrowing systems in 1936, which served 7,500 consumers over 3,000 miles of line, the coverage of the REA increased to the point where, in 1973, over 1,000 borrowers operated 1,766,701 miles of line and distributed electrical energy to 7,457,123 consumers.[18] During this same year, although the cooperatives controlled only a small portion of total installed generating capacity in the United States, they produced slightly more than 32 billion kilowatt hours and sold over 6 percent of all electrical energy. These utility systems purchased 71 percent of their wholesale power requirements—most of it from the government segment but a large portion from investor-owned companies. Only 67 of the 1,046 borrowers produced all or part of their energy requirements. This took place through a series of 216 generating plants comprised of 20 hydro, 141 internal combustion, and 55 steam-electric facilities. While the latter type of plant was small in number, it accounted for 94.5 percent of the total kilowatt hours generated.

The original REA commitment of supplying rural Americans with electric energy was accomplished by promoting the formation of small distribution systems which purchased power at wholesale rates from already existing utilities in their geographical areas. As these systems prospered, however, a number decided to construct their own generating and transmission (G&T) cooperatives in order to be less dependent upon outside sources for power. Although REA has been somewhat more restrictive in making loans to G&T systems, by 1973 cumulative borrowing for generation and transmission facilities amounted to over $3.6 billion or nearly 38 percent of total loans.[19] Whereas distribution borrowers from REA had over 85 percent of their total electric plant in distribution facilities, power supply borrowers' electric plant included only 7 percent in distribution facilities and nearly 81 percent in production and transmission equipment (see Table 2.6).

In addition to building their own power generating facilities, cooperatives began combining together as well as with investor-owned and municipal systems in joint ventures. For example, Central Iowa Power Cooperative and Corn Belt Power Cooperative joined with Iowa Electric Light and Power in the Duane Arnold Energy Center near Cedar Rapids—a 550-megawatt nuclear plant. This facility is 70 percent owned by the latter with the remainder held by the two cooperatives.[20] Additional cooperative joint ventures are taking place in Vermont, Maine, and Colorado. As the financing of large generating plants by individual systems becomes more difficult, the trend toward cooperation among various utilities will almost surely accelerate.

## COORDINATION

Virtually all of the principal electric utility systems in the United States are interconnected with nearby systems to make large integrated webs. The purpose of interconnection and coordination is twofold: 1) to provide more reliable service, and 2) achieve a reduction in costs. The latter goal is accomplished in a number of ways. One of these involves the construction of large generating

## TABLE 2.6

### Electric Plant in Service Reported by REA Borrowers, 1973
### (millions of dollars)

| Electric Plant in Service | Distribution Borrowers | | Power Supply Borrowers | |
|---|---|---|---|---|
| | Amount | Percent | Amount | Percent |
| Number of bor- rowers reporting | 925 | — | 40 | — |
| Total Electric Plant in Service | 6,824 | 100.0 | 1,708 | 100.0 |
| Intangible | 2 | a | 2 | 0.1 |
| Steam pro- duction | 49 | 0.7 | 732 | 42.9 |
| Hydraulic production | 14 | 0.2 | 9 | 0.5 |
| Other pro- duction | 46 | 0.7 | 61 | 3.6 |
| Transmission | 292 | 4.3 | 577 | 33.8 |
| Distribution | 5,811 | 85.2 | 119 | 7.0 |
| General | 535 | 7.9 | 61 | 3.6 |
| Purchased or sold | 1 | a | b | a |
| Leased to others | 15 | 0.2 | 62 | 3.6 |
| Held for future use | 2 | a | 2 | 0.1 |
| Acquisition ad- justments | 14 | 0.2 | (15)[c] | (0.9)[c] |
| Not classified | 43 | 0.6 | 97 | 5.7 |

[a]Less than 0.05 percent.
[b]Less than $500,000.
[c]Negative figure.

*Source*: U.S. Department of Agriculture, Rural Electrification Administration, *1973 Annual Statistical Report: REA Bulletin 1-1* (Washington: U.S. Department of Agriculture, 1974), p. 11.

plants which take advantage of economies of scale but result in excess capacity for a single utility. With proper coordination an alternating construction schedule can yield surplus capacity for one utility which can be used by one or more other systems. As the excess is used up, another plant comes on-line so that the seller-buyer arrangement is modified or reversed. A refinement of this technique, which yields similar results, is the unit-sale concept. Under this arrangement a utility builds a plant which is larger than its immediate needs require—again to take advantage of economies of scale—and sells a specific amount of the surplus capacity of the unit to nearby systems. While the unit-sale arrangement limits the purchaser to the availability of power from a specific unit, a modification is sometimes used whereby the supplier sells firm capacity for one or a number of years.

Another type of coordination which has received increasing popularity in recent years is the joint ownership of plants. The reduced availability of acceptable plant sites and the increasing cost and complexity of mammoth new generating equipment have prompted a number of electric utility systems to cooperate in the planning, construction, and output of large-scale facilities.[21] In the early joint ventures each utility held title to a specific portion of the plant and was authorized to its share of idle capacity in addition to its allotment of capacity and output. Currently, most such enterprises are with utilities in a like planning organization or power pool. Between 1968 and 1975, nearly 27,600 megawatts of generating capacity coming on-line were jointly owned and shared by members of formal power pools.[22]

Because of various difficulties and preferences, the joint ownership of transmission facilities is much less common than similar ventures in generating plants. There has, however, been some interest in cooperative efforts in bulk transmission.

Cost savings among utilities can be effected by seasonal capacity exchanges when peak loads between various systems or groups occur in different seasons of the year. While these exchanges generally take place between pools or regions, rather than between systems within the same region, the savings from eliminating the duplication of peak generating capacity can be significant.

One of the most expensive ingredients in maintaining the reliability of a system is providing sufficient reserve capacity to compensate for such things as errors in forecasting, delays in construction schedules, and down-time in equipment. If each utility was required to furnish all of its own reserve capacity the costs would be especially high since, hopefully, this capacity would remain unused most of the time. With coordinating organizations, formal arrangements can be undertaken so that the reserve margin is apportioned among the members. This sharing of reserve margins can be accomplished by having each member maintain a specified minimum capacity reserve, generally a percentage of peak load. Alternatively, the same goal can be attained by sharing existing installed generating capacity on an equalized reserve basis. Under the latter method, the reserve capacity of all the members is shared proportionately by each with those having capacity deficiencies reimbursing others who maintain surplus facilities.

Following the 1965 power failure in the Northeast, utilities attached increasing importance to planning and coordination on a regional scale. Outages during the failure established that a relatively large interconnected region could be seriously affected by malfunctions within an individual system. Initial reaction resulted in the establishment of the Northeast Power Coordinating Council, comprising one Canadian and two New York systems, whose aim was to improve the adequacy and reliability of bulk power supply. After expanding the number of these regional councils to five by the end of 1967, the electric utility industry formed the National Electric Reliability Council in June 1968 (see Figure 2.2). The Council is comprised of nine regional organizations and its purposes include reviewing regional and interregional activities on reliability, exchanging information on planning and operating matters, and facilitating the development of interregional reliability arrangements.[23] Although the individual councils have a review and approval role in matters involving bulk power facilities, they do not function as a decision-making authority in the planning or installation of such items.

## FIGURE 2.2

### National Electric Reliability Councils

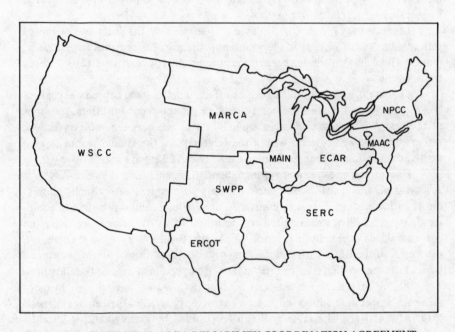

ECAR    - EAST CENTRAL AREA RELIABILITY COORDINATION AGREEMENT
MAIN     - MID-AMERICA INTERPOOL NETWORK
MAAC   - MID-ATLANTIC AREA COUNCIL
MARCA  -MID-CONTINENT AREA RELIABILITY COORDINATION AGREEMENT
NPCC    -NORTHEAST POWER COORDINATING COUNCIL
SERC     -SOUTHEASTERN ELECTRIC RELIABILITY COUNCIL
SWPP    -SOUTHWEST POWER POOL
ERCOT  -ELECTRIC RELIABILITY COUNCIL OF TEXAS
WSCC    -WESTERN SYSTEMS COORDINATING COUNCIL

*Source*: U.S. Federal Power Commission, *1974 Annual Report* (Washington: U.S. Government Printing Office, 1975), p. 21.

# REGULATION

During the first half century of their existence, electric utilities were regulated by state and local authorities. As various systems combined and grew internally, however, the need for more comprehensive control developed. This was especially true for the large investor-owned utilities which spanned state boundaries and made local regulation more difficult. While the primary responsibility for regulation of the electric utilities has remained under the auspices of state commissions, various federal policies have evolved during the last 45 years, leaving a clear imprint upon the industry.

## Federal Influence

Initial federal direction of the electric utility industry was incorporated into the Federal Water Power Act of 1920, which provided for a commission to license hydroelectric projects making use of waterways subject to federal jurisdiction. Subsequent legislation instituted supervision by a number of agencies, including the Federal Power Commission (FPC), the Securities and Exchange Commission, the Atomic Energy Commission, and the Environmental Protection Agency.

The Federal Power Act of 1935 made it the responsibility of the Federal Power Commission to assure"...an abundant supply of electric energy throughout the United States with the greatest possible economy and with regard to the proper utilization and conservation of natural resources."[24] While the act applied only to investor-owned utilities, the concept of cheap electrical power for consumers was, for the most part, amplified to cover other segments of the industry as well. In order to place the above legislation into effect, the FPC was given the responsibility to regulate interstate wholesale rates and services and to manage activities, reports, and accounts of corporate systems under its jurisdiction. While the commission has collected and disseminated what at times seems like overwhelming amounts of information, and while it has provided overall guidance to the industry, critics of its leadership do exist. Perhaps one of the most telling arguments is that the FPC has been too conservative in the interpretation of its delegated responsibilities. More specifically, areas of concern have centered on siting and rate design.[25]

Regulation by the Securities and Exchange Commission (SEC) is a product of both the Public Utility Holding Company Act of 1935 and the Securities and Exchange Commission Act of 1933. Under the former, the SEC regulates the types of operations of holding companies and their subsidiaries, while the 1935 act extends the province of regulation to all public utilities and involves the registration and issuance of debt and equity securities. The combination of the two acts allows the commission to direct the affairs of utilities with respect to mergers, security issuances, accounting, service company arrangements, and intercompany transactions. Since the commission is instrumental in deciding which types of subsidiaries are allowed to exist and what consolidations are permitted to take place, it plays an important part in determining the structure of the industry.

The Atomic Energy Act of 1954 delegated to the U.S. Atomic Energy Commission (AEC) all regulatory powers over the construction and operation of all nuclear reactors. In the process of bringing a nuclear plant on-line, a utility must acquire both a construction permit and an operating license.

An application for a construction permit and an environmental impact statement must be filed and approved before any permanent plant construction may ordinarily take place. These documents contain information on the type of reactor which is proposed and an assessment of the proposed site with respect to geology, seismology, hydrology, heterology, topography, and population centers. If this information is found satisfactory by the AEC and other regulatory agencies, the National Environmental Policy Act of 1969 then requires a public hearing before an Atomic Safety and Licensing Board to review environmental matters.

After construction has commenced and the research and development and principal design items are completed, the utility is eligible to apply for a operating license. Further review by the AEC and the Advisory Committee on Reactor Safeguards, plus the possibility of a second public hearing, is then necessary before the operating license can be issued. In addition to this license, personnel operating a nuclear facility are required to obtain licenses from the AEC.[26]

Under a government reorganization plan made effective in December of 1970, the Environmental Protection Agency (EPA) was established to administer the major federal pollution control programs which had previously been scattered among a number of separate agencies. EPA regulatory authority spans a wide spectrum and includes establishing and enforcing environmental standards for water quality, air quality, and radioactive emissions. (The setting of radiation standards has been the province of the EPA since 1970.)

## Rate Regulation

Private and public electric utilities can be subject to the controls of numerous regulatory bodies. This is especially important for the investor-owned segment of the industry, where most basic rate regulation occurs at the state and local level, while certain aspects are under the jurisdiction of the federal government or the courts. For example, the Federal Power Commission has authority over wholesale distribution from investor-owned utilities which accounts for approximately 10 percent of the revenues of this sector.[27]

While decisions by regulatory commissions are subject to review by the courts, the *Hope Natural Gas* case ruling by the United States Supreme Court inferred that the commissions could retain relatively wide discretion in rate-making, subject to the ability of the firm to maintain its financial integrity and attract sufficient amounts of capital to serve the public interest. In this case the Court stated:

> Rates which enable the company to operate successfully, to maintain its financial integrity, to attract capital, and to compensate investors for the risks assumed certainly cannot be condemned as invalid, even though they might produce only a meager return on the so-called 'fair value' rate base.[28]

In other words, the interest of the Court lay not so much in the methodology of rate-making, but rather in the end result.

Regardless of the supervisory body or the manner in which control is exercised, the return to a utility is a function of three variables: the valuation of assets included in the rate base, deductions which are allowed from operating revenues, and the percentage rate of return that is permitted. It is the combination of these three and not any individual factor which determines the end result.

The method of valuing utility assets has evolved through a number of concepts including original cost, reproduction cost, and fair value. Unless the return on assets is adjusted accordingly, the valuation method is especially important during a period of rapid inflation, but of less consequence with stable prices. With the *Hope* case allowing for more flexibility in rate-base judgment, commissions have moved toward one of three methodologies:[29]

1) Fifteen states calculate the rate base upon book value or original cost less depreciation.
2) Twelve states use replacement cost or present value in an attempt to calculate "fair values."
3) Eighteen states use no strict formula although they do not abandon the principle of the rate-base method.

Deductions from operating revenues are generally grouped into one of three categories: depreciation, operating expenses, and taxes. All of these are subject to various interpretations by interested parties, and commissions can effectively prohibit many types of expenditures by disallowing them for rate-making purposes.

The rate of return is defined as the amount of revenues left after accounting for operating expenses divided by the amount of assets included in the rate base. While there is no general agreement as to exactly what the percentage rate of return should be, the Supreme Court established in the *Hope* case that, "...the return to the equity owner should be commensurate with risks on investments in other enterprises having corresponding risks."[30] With public service commissions subject to the political pressures common to most other social organizations, however, the process of attempting to determine an equitable rate of return has not always been dictated by economic factors alone.[31] The result has been relatively wide variations in percentage returns to stockholders over time and between different utilities.

## METHODS OF PRODUCING POWER

As consumers increased their use of electrical energy and the electric utilities responded by doubling capacity every ten years, the composition of primary energies used to generate power was altered. As displayed in Table 2.7, fossil fuels—coal, oil, and gas—have been the major sources of primary energy for generating facilities over the past 45 years. From nearly 66 percent

## TABLE 2.7

### Primary Energy Sources for Generating Electricity, 1930-73 (percent)

| Year | Coal | Nuclear | Oil | Gas | Hydro |
|------|------|---------|------|------|-------|
| 1930 | 55.8 | — | 3.1 | 6.9 | 34.2 |
| 1935 | 48.0 | — | 4.2 | 7.6 | 40.3 |
| 1940 | 54.6 | — | 4.4 | 7.7 | 33.4 |
| 1945 | 51.7 | — | 3.5 | 8.9 | 35.9 |
| 1950 | 47.1 | — | 10.3 | 13.5 | 29.2 |
| 1955 | 55.1 | — | 6.8 | 17.4 | 20.7 |
| 1960 | 53.6 | — | 6.1 | 21.0 | 19.3 |
| 1965 | 54.5 | — | 6.1 | 21.0 | 18.4 |
| 1966 | 54.1 | — | 6.9 | 22.0 | 17.0 |
| 1967 | 52.6 | — | 7.4 | 21.8 | 18.2 |
| 1968 | 52.5 | — | 7.8 | 22.9 | 16.7 |
| 1969 | 49.0 | 1.0 | 9.6 | 23.1 | 17.3 |
| 1970 | 46.2 | 1.4 | 11.9 | 24.3 | 16.2 |
| 1971 | 44.3 | 2.3 | 13.5 | 23.3 | 16.5 |
| 1972 | 44.1 | 3.1 | 15.6 | 21.5 | 15.6 |
| 1973 | 45.9 | 4.5 | 16.8 | 18.2 | 14.7 |

Sources: U.S. Department of Commerce, Bureau of the Census, *Historical Statistics of the United States: Colonial Times to 1957,* Series S 15-35 and S 44-69 (Washington: U.S. Government Printing Office), p. 507; and idem, *Statistical Abstract of the United States, 1973* (Washington: U.S. Government Printing Office), p. 509.

of total energy sources in 1930, these three fuels increased their contribution to slightly over 79 percent in 1955, and then remained at around 80 percent through 1973. Of the three, coal has been the most important throughout the period, although it began a gradual decline in relative usage during the mid-1960s. While coal was in relative decline, the use of oil in steam plants was rapidly increasing. During the ten-year period, 1963-73, oil-fired plants tripled in relative usage from 5.5 percent to 16.8 percent of total primary energy sources. Gas increased its relative position prior to 1960 and remained at approximately 20 percent of total sources throughout the 1960s and early 1970s. Hydroelectric power declined in importance as the increasing demand for electricity far outstripped the ability to construct new hydroelectric facilities at a fixed number of viable sites. An increasing number of nuclear plants began coming on-line in the early 1970s and contributed a rising (although to many, a disappointingly small) portion of electrical output.

As the availability and price structure of the primary energy sources undergo changes in future years, the composition of the generation mix in producing electricity will continue to draw an increasing portion of the burden away from both hydroelectric and fossil-fuel facilities. Among the fossil fuels, coal will persist as the primary energy source. Although it should decline in importance relative to all sources in generating electricity, it will increase in relation to other fossil fuels. Hydroelectric energy will continue its declining significance in the generation mix. A 1973 projection of the generating mix by the Task Force on Utility Fuels Requirements of the Federal Power Commission is displayed in Figure 2.3.

## Hydroelectric Power

Hydroelectric power is produced at both conventional plants and pumped-storage facilities. In the former, dams are used to harness waterways which power turbines and electric generators. These facilities use streamflows as received at the plant site, and reservoirs to store water to meet seasonal or intermediate needs. Pumped storage projects include both facilities which utilize energy from water that has previously been pumped to a reservoir at a higher elevation, and developments which produce electric power from both pumped storage and natural drainage. In these facilities, water is pumped during off-peak periods, and then allowed to fall back and power turbines to meet load requirements under high demand conditions. Pumped storage plants require approximately three kilowatt hours of pumping energy to provide two kilowatt hours of generation.[32] Hydro facilities, while increasing in aggregate capacity over the years, have supplied a diminishing portion of total electrical output. This decline in relative importance is primarily due to the scarcity of suitable hydroelectric sites near major load centers. In addition, some of the most favorable sites

# FIGURE 2.3

## Projected Energy Source Generation Mix, 1974-90

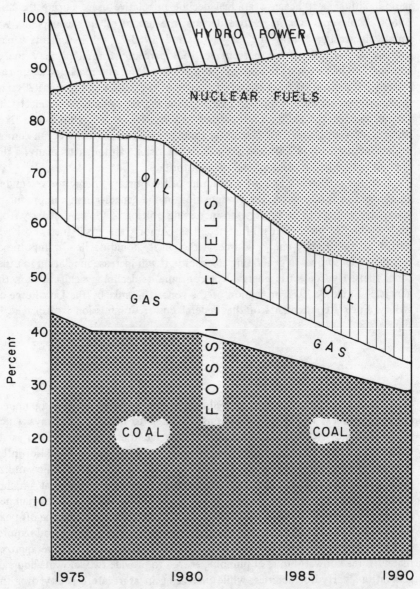

Source: U.S. Federal Power Commission, *Report of the Task Force on Utility Fuels Requirements* (August 1973), p. 37.

remaining are, by their nature, also desirable in an undeveloped state for their aesthetic beauty.[33]

By most standards a hydro plant provides a superior method of power production. It requires no natural fuel input, operational and maintenance expenses are relatively low, and the working life is long. In addition, hydro facilities have the ability to be started quickly with rapid changes in output, and forced outages are infrequent and generally of short duration. While these plants are free of most of the environmental effects associated with steam-plant operations, they do require large amounts of land use, and the investment cost per kilowatt hour of capacity is considerably higher than for thermal-electric plants.

The majority of hydroelectric plants are located in the Pacific and mountain states, where the terrain is most suitable for such facilities. For example, in the 11 western states comprising the Western Systems Coordinating Council, the Federal Power Commission estimated that nearly 46 percent of electric demand in 1974 could be expected to be supplied from water-driven turbines.[34] While these states possess the majority of hydro facilities already in operation, they also contain most of the remaining potential areas which would be compatible for further development. These two regions, when combined with Alaska, incorporate three times as much undeveloped capacity as the rest of the United States.[35]

Most hydro units are owned by investor-owned utilities. Since many of these plants are older, however, their combined capacity of 20.8 million kilowatts is considerably less than for a smaller number of facilities which are federally owned. A significant number of hydroelectric plants are also held by nonfederal public utilities.

## Conventional Steam-Electric Power

Conventional steam plants burn coal, oil, or natural gas to produce heat which is used in converting water to high pressure steam. This steam pressure is then utilized in powering turbines which spin generators. These fossil-fuel steam-electric plants have dominated power production in the industry, and in 1973 contributed nearly 81 percent of total generation.

Significant improvements were incorporated into the design and construction of fossil-fuel plants over the years. Increased automation, more efficient fuel use, and larger unit size to take advantage of economies of scale, resulted in continuing reductions in production costs through the mid-1960s. Since 1966, however, the escalation of construction and operating costs has not been compensated for by improved technology.

In 1930, the average size of all steam-electric units was 20 megawatts. By 1955, when larger units began to come on-line in significant numbers, the average unit size had jumped to 35 megawatts and the largest unit had increased to 300 megawatts. Subsequent years showed a continuous progression of larger units until 1974, when four 1,300-megawatt units were in operation and a 1,500 megawatt unit was projected to come on-line in 1983.[36] Even if future units do not increase greatly in size, the average unit size will continue to expand as older and smaller units are retired. While unit size increased, plant size also grew. In 1972, the largest steam-electric plant in the United States was the seven-unit Sammis plant of Ohio Edison with 2,889 megawatts of capacity.[37] In 1948, the largest plant had a capacity of 881 megawatts and there was only one other plant with a capacity of over 500 megawatts.

Although the composition of fossil-fuels for steam plants changed over the years, coal has continued to provide the largest share of energy input (see Table 2.8). In 1973, this fuel comprised slightly over 52 percent of all fossil-fuel energy used by electric utilities, and over the past 15 years it consistantly supplied between 50 and 65 percent of fossil-fuel generation. In the late 1950s and early 1960s, the apparent advantages of nuclear energy combined with increasing environmental awareness by the public, caused many utilities to downgrade the long-term importance of coal. With the emergence of events in the late 1960s and early 1970s, however, increased emphasis was being devoted to the planning and construction of coal-fired plants. Among the causes of this "rebirth" were delays and rising costs of nuclear facilities, and the realization that supplies of petroleum and natural gas would become increasingly inadequate. While a number of major problems areas—mainly environmental—remain, the estimated 200 billion tons of recoverable reserves of coal in the United States virtually dictate that this fuel will remain the dominant source of fossil-fuel energy in electric power generation for many decades.[38]

Although oil has seen a rapid increase in use during the past two decades, the changing world political and economic climate, combined with the decline of oil production in the United States, prohibit this fossil-fuel from serving a major role in the long-term energy picture of electric utilities. With nearly two-thirds of the world's proved oil reserves in the Middle East and North Africa, and the lack of new discoveries in the United States, increased burning of oil by fossil-fuel plants will be at the expense of increased dependence on foreign sources. Even the rapid development of Alaskan oil will only offset further production declines from other domestic sources. Due to the time involved in bringing increased nuclear and coal facilities into production, however, oil must play a very important part in fueling electric generation over the intermediate term.

The relative importance of oil as an energy source for utilities varies in different parts of the country. Most residual fuel oil use is concentrated in areas near refineries or close to water transport facilities since it cannot be easily moved by pipeline. Eastern states are especially dependent on oil-fired plants and the New England area derives the vast majority of electricity from these facilities.

## TABLE 2.8

### Consumption of Fossil Fuels by Electric Utilities, 1930-73

| Year | Coal | Oil | Gas | Equivalent* |
|------|------|-----|------|-------------|
| 1930 | 40 | 9 | 119 | 48 |
| 1935 | 33 | 11 | 124 | 41 |
| 1940 | 51 | 16 | 180 | 63 |
| 1945 | 75 | 20 | 326 | 93 |
| 1950 | 92 | 75 | 629 | 138 |
| 1955 | 144 | 75 | 1,153 | 207 |
| 1960 | 177 | 85 | 1,724 | 266 |
| 1965 | 245 | 115 | 2,321 | 369 |
| 1966 | 266 | 141 | 2,609 | 412 |
| 1967 | 274 | 161 | 2,746 | 432 |
| 1968 | 298 | 189 | 3,148 | 481 |
| 1969 | 311 | 241 | 3,488 | 524 |
| 1970 | 321 | 336 | 3,932 | 583 |
| 1971 | 328 | 396 | 3,993 | 618 |
| 1972 | 351 | 494 | 3,979 | 672 |
| 1973 | 388 | 557 | 3,605 | 724 |

*Converted as 25 million Btu equal to one ton of coal.

*Note*: Coal and total coal equivalent in millions of short tons, oil in millions of barrels, and gas in billions of cubic feet.

*Sources*: U.S. Department of Commerce, Bureau of the Census, *Historical Statistics of the United States: Colonial Times to 1957*, Series S 36-43 (Washington: U.S. Government Printing Office), pp. 507-08, and idem, *Statistical Abstract of the United States, 1973* (Washington: U.S. Government Printing Office), p. 512.

For consumers, natural gas possesses nearly all the attributes of an ideal fossil fuel. It is relatively cheap, clean burning, and at one time so abundant as to be flared at the wellhead. Currently, however, the supply of this fuel falls short of meeting nonutility needs, let alone the expanding demand from electric utilities. While utilities may increase their use of this energy source during the remainder of the present decade, the expansion will be relatively small and a decline in electric production from gas-fired plants will probably follow.[39] As with the other fossil fuels, the burning of gas for steam-electric generation will continue to vary by geographical region. It will quite probably maintain its dominance in California and in the West South Central region.

## Nuclear Power

Nuclear power plants operate in a manner similar to fossil-fuel plants in that high-pressure steam is used to power turbines and generators. In this type of facility, nuclear power, rather than the burning of fossil fuels, is used in converting water to steam. There are currently two principal types of reactors in use in the United States: the boiling-water reactor and the pressurized-water reactor. In the former, heat in the reactor core is used to generate steam that is passed directly through a turbogenerator. Since radioactivity is present in the steam, shielding of components with which the steam comes into contact is necessary. In a pressurized-water reactor the steam generated in the reactor core is separated from the turbine by a heat exchanger. Radioactive steam in the primary loop transfers its heat to a secondary loop through the heat exchanger, and steam in the secondary loop is then used to power the turbine. In this type of system radioactivity is confined to the primary side of the steam generator so that the turbine steam system is not radioactive. Babcock and Wilcox, Westinghouse, and Combustion Engineering are the primary U.S. manufacturers of pressurized-water reactors, while General Electric produces boiling-water reactors. In addition, Gulf General Atomic is manufacturing high-temperature gas reactors.

Although nuclear plants generated less than 5 percent of total electric power in 1973, in the early 1970s more than half the generating capacity ordered was nuclear.[40] As these plants begin coming on-line (current lead time to commercial operation runs eight to ten years) the contribution of nuclear energy will reach more significant proportions. Nuclear plants have run into a number of problems which have kept their contribution below forecasted levels. Among these are escalating costs and construction delays relating to safety concerns and possible environmental harm.

Current light-water reactors make inefficient use of uranium fuel. Each type effectively utilizes only U-235, which comprises less than 1 percent of natural uranium. As such, if these plants are the sole components of forecasted nuclear capacity, low-cost uranium resources in the United States will prove sufficient for only a few decades.[41] A possible answer to this problem is commercial development of the liquid-metal fast breeder reactor (LMFBR)—a project backed by the utility industry, the Atomic Energy Commission, and the Federal Power Commission. The LMFBR uses sodium as a coolant and is fueled with a mixture of plutonium and uranium-238. Since the latter is more abundant than U-235, and since the breeder produces more plutonium than it consumes, the use of this reactor would stretch the nation's uranium resources to hundreds of years. Unfortunately, the LMFBR has run into numerous problems including rapidly escalating costs and criticism from environmentalists. In June of 1975, the Energy Research and Development Administration further delayed development by calling for a study to determine if the reactor is even needed.[42]

## Alternative Production Methods

The above-mentioned methods of electric power production provide virtually all of the base-load generating capacity in the United States. However, a number of additional types of facilities are currently in use or present the possibility of commercially viable systems in future years.

Gas turbines and diesels are commonly used to meet peaking requirements or as reserves in case normal generating capacity fails. In some cases diesels are used both for base loads and peaking demands of smaller systems. Although energy costs are relatively high with these systems, this disadvantage is offset by lower capital and labor costs, the ability to start and stop quickly, and satisfactory operation at partial loads.

The possibility of an expanding use of geothermal energy to produce electric power exists primarily in the western United States. This energy exists where hot portions of the earth's crust are close enough to underground water to produce steam. Where heat is concentrated into limited volume, the energy can be economically used to power turbines and generators. Most of the potential geothermal energy is concentrated in federally controlled lands and the only working facility in the United States is the 192-megawatt "Geyser" complex north of San Francisco, which is operated by Pacific Gas and Electric. One projection estimates there will be 7,000 megawatts of geothermal capacity by 1985.[43]

A number of alternative methods of power production are currently in the experimental or design stage, but because of technological or economic limitations, none are commercially feasible on a large scale. These include fuel cells, magnetohydrodynamics, electrogasdynamics, thermonic generation, thermoelectric generation, solar generation, and fusion. While the last mode of energy generation is still far removed from practical application, its tremendous possibilities lead many to believe that it is perhaps the ultimate source of power, and that its development deserves additional consideration and dollars.[44]

# TRANSMISSION AND DISTRIBUTION

As ever larger generating plants have been built to supply an expanding demand for electrical energy, the need for new transmission construction has kept pace. Since nuclear plants are generally located away from population centers and since many new fossil-fuel generating units are being built close to fuel sources rather than near load centers, the importance of an efficient transmission system is evident.

Currently, between 3 percent and 5 percent of the power transmitted on high voltage transmission systems is consumed in transmission losses, and the annual growth in these losses is the equivalent of a new 1,000-megawatt generating plant.[45] Since the most important factors in these line losses are distance and voltage, there has been a tendency to construct higher-voltage transmission systems to offset the increased distance over which power is transferred. Research is currently underway on the development of 1,200-kilovolt lines which are expected to incur only one-half the losses of present 765-kilovolt lines. In addition to reducing losses, the higher-voltage lines allow greater load-carrying capability since capacity increases as the square of the voltage. The result has been a more efficient use of rights-of-way and improved interconnection to permit greater reliability.

Nearly all transmission in the United States is by means of alternating current, although an 800-kilovolt direct-current line with 1,400 megawatts of capacity was put into service between northern Oregon and southern California in 1970. While losses in direct-current lines are only about 65 percent of those in alternating-current lines, the additional losses incurred in converting from alternating to direct current and then back again usually more than offset the greater efficiency of the former.

Study is underway on transmission systems with conductors cooled to a sufficiently low temperature to result in significantly lower resistivity. It appears that the power required for refrigeration may cancel savings in line losses. In any case, meaningful application is in the distant future.[46]

Distribution facilities are used to subdivide high-voltage current from transmission lines and carry it to individual customers at suitable voltages. These include transformers to reduce voltages, primary and secondary distribution lines, customer service transformers, and connecting services. Distribution systems account for 40 percent of total electric utility investment[47] and 40 percent of total power system losses. Most of the latter occurs in the distribution transformers.

## ENVIRONMENTAL CONSIDERATIONS

As is the case with nearly all types of industrial production, electric power generation and its supporting activities create environmental impacts in water quality, air quality, land use, and solid waste.[48] The type and severity of degradation depends upon a number of factors including the method of production and size of operation. A summary of the comparative environmental impacts at various types of installations is displayed in Table 2.9.

Hydroelectric facilities have the least overall detrimental effect on the environment. The primary problem is that these plants require the flooding of vast areas of land which may be valuable in an economic or scenic sense. In addition, since the generating units may be a considerable distance from major load centers, many miles of high-voltage power lines are required.

## TABLE 2.9

### Comparative Environmental Impacts of 1,000-Megawatt Electric Energy Systems

| System | Air Emissions | Water discharges | Solid Waste | Land Use | Potential for Large-Scale Disaster |
|---|---|---|---|---|---|
| Coal | | | | | |
| Deep-mined | 5 | 5 | 3 | 3 | Mine accidents |
| Surface-mined | 5 | 5 | 5 | 5 | Landslides |
| Oil | | | | | |
| Onshore | 3 | 3 | 1 | 2 | Massive spill on land from blow-out or pipeline rupture |
| Offshore | 3 | 4 | 1 | 1 | Massive spill on water from blow-out or pipeline rupture |
| Imports | 2 | 4 | 1 | 1 | Massive oil spill from tanker accident |
| Natural gas | 1 | 2 | 0 | 2 | Pipeline explosion |
| Nuclear | 1 | 3 | 4 | 2 | Core meltdown, radiological health accidents |

*Note*: Assumes operation at .75 load factor with low levels of environmental controls or with generally prevailing controls.
Severity rating key: 5 = serious, 4 = significant, 3 = moderate, 2 = small, 1 = negligible, 0 = none.
*Source*: Council on Environmental Quality, *Energy and the Environment: Electric Power* (Washington: U.S. Government Printing Office, 1973), p. 14.

33

Conventional steam-electric plants, especially coal-fired units, produce numerous types of environmental problems. The most obvious residuals are those which pollute the air. These include particulate matter, hydrocarbons, nitrogen oxides, sulfur oxides, and carbon monoxide. Coal-burning electric power plants alone are responsible for 43 percent of the sulfur emissions in the United States.[49] In a relative sense, oil, and especially natural gas, are much cleaner-burning fuels.

All steam-electric plants produce waste heat which is dissipated through the stacks or released into rivers or lakes in the water that flows through the condenser. Thermal efficiency for fossil-fuel plants varies from 30 to 40 percent, and currently the electric power industry is responsible for about three-fourths of the total U.S. use of cooling water.[50] The effects of thermal discharges are not fully understood and can vary widely depending upon the size of the receiving body of water, the uses to which the water is put, the climate, and the rate and constancy of thermal discharge. However, the raising of ambient water temperature may alter the natural balance of aquatic life and result in the degradation of lakes, bays, estuaries, and rivers.

While nuclear plants discharge approximately 50 percent more waste heat into water than comparatively sized fossil-fuel plants, they produce no similar air pollutants. Rather, they result in low-level radioactive releases. Although this was once considered to be the major drawback of nuclear reactors, recent concern has centered on the disposal of radioactive wastes and the possibility of loss-of-coolant accidents. No long-term solution has yet been found for the former and, in spite of numerous safety precautions, a potential loss-of-coolant accident is a hazard the public will, at present, have to assume.

Aesthetic considerations have become an increasingly important aspect of electric power production as plants, transmission and distribution systems, and supporting services have expanded in size. For example, the huge new cooling towers and transmission towers are scenic blights that power officials can do little to remedy. The former are required to alleviate thermal discharge problems and the latter cannot be feasibly placed underground.

## NOTES

1. U.S. Department of Commerce, Bureau of the Census, *Statistical Abstract of the United States* (Washington: U.S. Government Printing Office, various years).

2. See John C. Fisher, *Energy Crises in Perspective* (New York: John Wiley and Sons, 1974), Chapter 9.

3. "Private, Public Power Coexist Peacefully," *Electrical World* 181, no. 11 (June 1, 1974): 48.

4. U.S. Federal Power Commission, *1970 National Power Survey* (Washington: U.S. Government Printing Office, 1971), p. I-2-2.

5. Hunton, Williams, Gay and Gibson, National Economic Research Associates, and Debevoise and Liberman, "The Development and Structure of the Electric Utility Industry and the Impact of Government Policies," as reprinted in U.S. Congress, Senate, Committee on Interior and Insular Affairs, *Electric Utility Policy Issues,* 92nd Cong., pursuant to Senate Resolution 45, p. 42.

6. "The Fortune Directory of the 500 Largest Industrial Corporations," *Fortune* 91, no. 5 (May 1975): 210.

7. U.S. Federal Power Commission, *Statistics of Publicly Owned Electric Utilities in the United States, 1971* (Washington: U.S. Government Printing Office, 1973), pp. 6, 11, and 66.

8. Ibid., p. 3a.

9. Ibid., p. 3.

10. Ibid., p. 44.

11. U.S. Department of Commerce, Bureau of the Census, *Statistical Abstract of the United States, 1974* (Washington: U.S. Government Printing Office).

12. Arnold R. Jones, "The Financing to TVA," *Law and Contemporary Problems* (Autumn 1961): 728.

13. For example see *Tennessee Valley Authority Act,* Section 10. (49 Stat. 1076, 16 U.S.C. Sec. 831 H-1.)

14. Hunton, Williams, Gay and Gibson, op. cit., p. 41.

15. U.S. General Accounting Office, Comptroller General of the United States, *Potential Curtailment of Electric Power Service by the Tennessee Valley Authority,* A report to Senator Bill Brock, November 4, 1974.

16. U.S. Department of Agriculture, Rural Electrification Administration, *Rural Lines: The Story of Cooperative Rural Electrification* (Washington: U.S. Government Printing Office, 1973), p. 4.

17. Ibid., p. 6.

18. U.S. Department of Agriculture, Rural Electrification Administration, *1973 Annual Statistical Report: REA Bulletin 1-1* (Washington: U.S. Department of Agriculture, 1974), p. 4.

19. Ibid., p. 1.

20. David A. Hamil, "Stepping Up the Pace in Financing," *Public Utilities Fortnightly* 95, no. 5 (February 27, 1975): 32.

21. For example, Niagara Mohawk recently combined with a number of utilities in building two large power plants. See The *Wall Street Journal,* June 4, 1975, p. 5.

22. U.S. Federal Power Commission, *1970 National Power Survey,* op. cit., p. I-17-25.

23. Ibid., p. I-17-14.

24. 16 United States Code B2A (a).

25. For example, see Edward Berlin, Charles Cicchetti, and William Gillen, "A Report to the Energy Policy Project of the Ford Foundation," *Perspective on Power* (Cambridge, Massachusetts: Ballinger Publishing Co., 1974), Chapter 4.

26. U.S. Federal Power Commission, *1970 National Power Survey,* op. cit., p. I-6-7.

27. Berlin et al., op. cit., p. 66.

28. *Federal Power Commission* v. *Hope Natural Gas Co.,* 320 U.S. 591(1944).

29. Berlin et al., op. cit., p. 62.

30. *Federal Power Commission* v. *Hope Natural Gas Co.*

31. See Martin Farris and Roy Sampson, *Public Utilities* (Boston: Houghton Mifflin, 1973), Chapter 8.

32. U.S. Federal Power Commission, *1970 National Power Survey*, op. cit., p. I-7-4.

33. For example, the battle between environmental groups and Pacific Northwest Power Company in U.S. Congress, Senate, Subcommittee on Parks and Recreation, *Hearings, Hells Canyon–Snake National River*, 92nd Cong., 1st Sess., 1971.

34. U.S. Federal Power Commission, *Report of the Task Force on Utility Fuels Requirements*, 1973, p. 32.

35. ———, *1974 Annual Report* (Washington: U.S. Government Printing Office, 1974), p. 87.

36. Ibid., p. 78.

37. U.S. Federal Power Commission, *Steam-Electric Plant Construction Cost and Annual Production Expenses* (Washington: U.S. Government Printing Office, 1974), p. 111.

38. ———, Technical Advisory Committee on Fuels, *Task Force Report on Fuels Availability*, 1973.

39. ———, *Report of the Task Force on Utility Fuels Requirements*, 1973, p. 23.

40. ———, *1974 Annual Report,* p. 14

41. Manson Benedict, "Electric Power From Nuclear Fission," *Science and Public Affairs* 27, no. 7 (September 1971): 12.

42. The *Wall Street Journal,* June 6, 1975, p. 4.

43. National Petroleum Council, *U.S. Energy Outlook* (December 1972).

44. See Samuel Glasstone, *Controlled Nuclear Fusion*, U.S. Atomic Energy Commission, Division of Technical Information (Washington: U.S. Government Printing Office, 1968); also, R.F. Post, "Fusion Power: The Uncertainty," *Science and Public Affairs* 27, no. 8 (October 1971).

45. U.S. Federal Power Commission, *Report of the Technical Advisory Committee on Conservation of Energy* (May 1974), Section V, p. 28.

46. Ibid., p. 31.

47. U.S. Federal Power Commission, *1970 National Power Survey*, op. cit., p. I-14-1.

48. For a more complete analysis of the environmental aspects of electric power production see, David L. Scott, *Pollution in the Electric Power Industry* (Lexington, Mass.: D.C. Heath and Co., 1973).

49. U.S. Congress, Joint Committee on Atomic Energy, *Hearings on Environmental Effects of Producing Electric Power*, 91st Cong., 1st Sess., 1969, p. 811.

50. U.S. Federal Power Commission, Technical Advisory Committee on Fuels, *Task Force Report on Environmental Considerations and Constraints*, 1973, p. 49.

# 3

Until recent years, the pricing actions of the electric utility industry were of little concern to the vast majority of consumers. The cost of electricity had fallen quite sharply from 1933 to the end of World War II, and declined more gradually from that point through the 1950s and 1960s. When adjusted for climbing prices in other sectors of the economy, the plunge in electric costs was even more dramatic (see Figure 3.1). The fall in the price of electricity to consumers during the last two decades was due not so much to a decline in rates; rates actually increased slightly for certain classes of users during a number of years. Rather, the reduction was fostered by the declining rate-block structure used by most electric utilities in pricing their product. Under this type of schedule, the cost per kilowatt hour declines when more electricity is used, even though the average bill increases. For example, from 1962 to 1969, the average cost of electricity to residential customers fell from 2.564¢ to 2.210¢ per kilowatt hour, while the average annual bill increased from slightly over $99 to nearly $138.[1] As consumers became more affluent and purchased an ever-widening array of electrically-powered devices, they progressed upward through the block structure, increasing their usage and total bills, while at the same time decreasing their average cost per kilowatt hour. A typical residential schedule is displayed in Table 3.1.

In 1970, however, rate increases were sufficiently large so that increased usage did not succeed in reducing average cost per kilowatt hour for residential, commercial, or industrial service. Subsequent years showed an even more dramatic reversal of the earlier trend. Rapidly rising fuel costs, inflated capital spending requirements, and environmental restrictions were chief among the villains of rising prices. In addition, if regulatory commissions had acted as swiftly as the utilities desired, the increases would have occurred much more rapidly.

## FIGURE 3.1

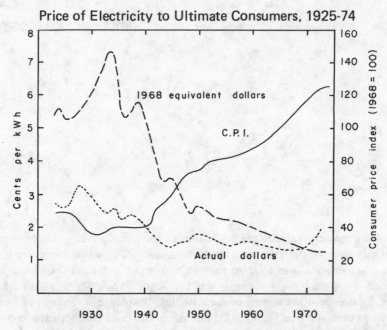

### Price of Electricity to Ultimate Consumers, 1925-74

*Source*: U.S. Federal Power Commission, *1970 National Power Survey* (Washington: U.S. Government Printing Office, 1971), p. I-19-2; and Standard and Poor, *Industry Surveys: Utilities-Electric* (New York: Standard and Poor, 1975), p. U-12.

## TABLE 3.1

### Typical Residential Rate Schedule

| Usage | Cost Per Unit (cents per kilowatt hour) |
|-------|------------------------------------------|
| First 100 kWh | 3.00 |
| Next 300 kWh | 2.50 |
| Next 500 kWh | 1.90 |
| Additional kWh | 1.80 |

*Source*: Compiled by the author.

While various regulating commissions have the authority to set rates for nearly all public utilities, the actual rate structure is many times established by the utility subject only to some maximum return or revenue figure as set by the commission. As a result, an intended sphere of influence of many commissions falls to the utilities by default. This abandonment by the commissions does not necessarily indicate, as many argue, that they serve only the interests of the utilities they are supposed to be regulating. Rather, in many instances the commissions are simply overextended and outgunned. Where rate increases were considerably less than utilities requested, the cause could frequently be traced to political pressure and consumer resistance.

Electric utilities typically segregate their customers into three major categories—residential, commercial, and industrial—and levy a different rate schedule against each. These users may, in turn, be divided into a number of various subcategories. In 1974, the average charge per kilowatt hour among relatively heavy users in each of the three classifications was 2.49¢, 3.21¢, and 2.60¢ respectively.[2] The term "heavy users" is somewhat misleading since nearly all big consumers in the residential category would be considered only small purchasers if they were in the industrial classification. Justification for price discrimination among the various categories is generally based upon cost of service, in that it may cost more to provide power to members of one classification than to others. Indeed, a similar argument is used as a defense of the declining block schedule within each grouping.

While consumption of kilowatt hours is generally the only variable taken into account in computing residential bills, nonresidential customers may be subject to further refinement. For example, since capacity which is built to meet peak demand periods but otherwise remains unused can be extremely expensive, large users are frequently billed according to a demand charge in addition to accounting for the actual quantity of kilowatt hours consumed. Under this type of demand schedule, the consumer with relatively steady usage will be rewarded with lower electric costs, while a highly variable load will be penalized. The purpose is to induce customers to even out their loads, or at least have them pay a penalty if they do not do so. In actual practice, this type of tariff system is only partially successful since a utility's unused capacity is a function of the entire system's load factor and not necessarily an individual customer's load factor. It could be the case that an attempt to even out the average load by an individual would actually result in a more erratic load in the aggregate. An example would be where a large user's slack demand coincided with the utility's peak demand. Any attempt by the individual to balance his load by transferring demand to the prime period of smaller usage would actually cause a greater peak load for the entire system.[3] Conversely, the opposite type of transfer would incur a penalty charge while actually benefiting the utility.

## NATURE OF PRICING

The economic principle of maximizing profits at the level of output where marginal revenue equals marginal cost is as appropriate for a monopolist such as an electric utility as it is for an oligopolist or a firm in a perfectly competitive market. Unfortunately, except in the case of the latter, the result of maximizing profits is an artifically high price with too little of the product being sold and an inadequate use of resources by the industry. To correct the misallocation of resources, the firm should use marginal cost pricing. However, this could, in turn, result in revenues which are either inadequate or too high. In the former case, deficits would ensue, and in the latter, public outrage. While the revenue problem could be overcome by public subsidies or taxation, this course of action has not been particularly popular, or even legal, with respect to privately owned utilities.

Perhaps an even greater difficulty in setting prices in conjunction with short-run marginal cost is the attempt to measure the latter variable. Many of the costs associated with electric power generation are external to the industry, such as pollution, and even the explicit costs are highly unstable.[4] Not only would the industry spend considerable money in continually providing cost data, but consumers would be equally occupied in the expensive and time-consuming process of trying to adjust to the variations.[5] A more practical pricing mechanism is long-run incremental cost which would not be subject to the erratic movements of short-run variables.

## THE COST FRAMEWORK

The capital intensive nature of the electric utilities is the most significant cost characteristic of the industry. The electric power companies not only require more capital per year than any other industry, but they also need more money invested in capital per dollar of revenue than any other manufacturing industry in the United States. Even the railroads and communication companies require only two-thirds the amount of assets per dollar of revenue as the electric utilities.[6] A comparison of the industry and other manufacturing sectors is displayed in Table 3.2.

The large amount of fixed assets required to generate and distribute electricity is instrumental to the financing, cost structure, and pricing policies of the industry. It precipitates large quantities of long-term debt, heavy fixed expenses in depreciation and interest, and an intense desire to sell sufficient amounts of power so that plant and equipment are kept in operation. This latter need is so strong that, in some cases, prices are designed to cover only a portion of average costs, although all of variable costs. Examples of customers facing this type of price schedule would be those on interruptable service or those whose use is during off-peak hours when excess capacity is available.

## TABLE 3.2

Asset to Revenue Ratios for Selected Manufacturing Industries, 1972

| Industry | Gross Plant per Dollar of Revenue | Net Plant per Dollar of Revenue |
|---|---|---|
| Electric utilities | 4.42 | 3.46 |
| Petroleum refining | 1.36 | 0.75 |
| Primary metals | 1.19 | 0.59 |
| Basic chemicals | 1.11 | 0.52 |
| Transportation equipment | 0.44 | 0.21 |
| All manufacturing | 0.60 | 0.31 |

*Source:* Hunton, Williams, Gay, and Gibson, "The Development and Structure of the Electric Utility Industry and the Impact of Government Policies," as reprinted in U.S. Congress, Senate, Committee on Interior and Insular Affairs, *Electric Utility Policy Issues*, 92nd Congress, 2nd Sess., 1974, pursuant to Senate Resolution 45, p. 84.

Electric utilities are subject to load cycles during nearly all time periods. Depending upon the geographical area of service and substitute energy availability, companies must have a ready supply of peak capacity for either summer or winter. For example, southern systems usually have seasonal peaks during the summer months while many utilities in the western United States experience maximum demand during winter months. In addition, electric companies must face load variations on both a weekly and daily basis. Weekly load cycles peak during weekdays leaving excess capacity during Saturday and Sunday, while swings in daily loads create maximum unused facilities during the early morning hours. Most companies serve peak loading requirements during the early evening. Variations in demand are a function not only of climate and weather, but also of the composition of residential, commercial, and industrial users and cycles of social activity.

The addition of customers that increases the peak load of a utility, but does not improve its load factor,* is expensive since it eventually forces the construction of new facilities. During a period of above-average inflation, the expansion will result in higher average costs and rising electric rates, since additions to plant and equipment cost considerably more per kilowatt of capacity

---

*Load factor is the ratio of the average load to the peak or maximum load during a period of time.

than the existing capital. During prior years, when price increases were relatively low, improved technology and economies of scale more than offset the burden of inflation and yielded a decreasing cost industry. Recently, however, this utopian set of factors has been replaced by a level of inflation against which the utilities have not been able to compensate.

Customers that improve a utility's load factor by coming on-line during off-peak hours result in comparatively low marginal costs for the company. The expense of generating additional power during periods of excess capacity is primarily composed of the cost of additional fuel. While this cost has increased substantially since 1970, it is still considerably less than fully allocated costs. The problem is that it is somewhat difficult to find customers that add to the load factor by consuming electricity only during off-peak hours. While altering the composition of customer classes (for example, adding an industrial base to a service area that is primarily residential) will increase off-peak usage, it will also probably increase peak-load requirements. If the industry creates new jobs, an influx of new residents may occur which will increase the maximum load even more.

Electric utilities have made some attempts at leveling their loads by applying different rate structures to various classes of customers. In addition, many companies with seasonal peaks have imposed rate schedules which are varied during the year. For example, a number of utilities with high peak loads in the summer increase their rates during those months. This can be done with across-the-board increases or by increasing the price of tail-end blocks only.

There has been less interest among utility executives in altering the price of electricity to track costs throughout the daily load cycle.[7] This, at first, seems somewhat surprising since it is the erratic nature of daily usage which produces the greatest variation in the cost of generating electricity.[8] One of the primary arguments against peak-load pricing is that it would require the installation of expensive metering equipment. For this reason many industry officials argue that it is cheaper and more feasible to improve load factors by promoting off-peak usage rather than by attempting to curtail peak loads through double metering. While at one time the problems of cost and technology were valid evidence against time-differentiated pricing, recent technological improvements in metering and increases in the cost of additional capacity have tended to give the argument less credence.

A number of public utility commissions have become interested in the concept of peak-load pricing and have instituted hearings on its inclusion in current rate structures. Central Vermont Public Service Corporation, for example, undertook implementation of the concept on a small sample of its customers. During the test period, the utility charged its experimental customers 103.4 mills per kilowatt hour during peak periods of 8 a.m. to 11 a.m. and 5 p.m. to 9 p.m., and 16.5 mills per kilowatt hour during the remaining off-peak hours.[9]

## Capital Costs

The escalation of capital costs in electric utility plant construction during recent years has been staggering. This is in contrast to stable or even declining plant costs per kilowatt of capacity during the 1950s and early 1960s. Beginning in the mid-1960s, the upward spiral had started. Cost increases occurred in nearly all categories of generating and delivering electricity to consumers, including production, transmission, and distribution.

*Plant Costs*

A 1967 study for the Atomic Energy Commission estimated light-water reactor plant costs for commercial operation in 1972 at $134 per kilowatt. Estimated costs for coal-fired plants with a similar time schedule were slightly over $100 per kilowatt.[10] Both of these estimates were calculated using constant 1967 prices. A more recent 1972 estimate on capital costs, including escalation, for plants commencing commercial operation in early 1983, has increased the costs to approximately $720 per kilowatt for a nuclear plant and $626 per kilowatt for a coal-fired facility.[11]

Although the decreasing cost of larger unit size has not been sufficient to offset the effects of inflation in recent years, economies of scale are still extremely important in the construction of new plants. Table 3.3 illustrates estimated economies of increasing unit size for a two-unit plant with commercial operation in 1981.

### TABLE 3.3

### Unit Capital Costs of Two-Unit Power Plants for 1981 Operation (dollars per kilowatt)

| Type of Plant | Unit Size (megawatts) | | | | |
|---|---|---|---|---|---|
| | 600 | 800 | 1,000 | 1,200 | 1,300 |
| Pressurized water reactor | 703 | 641 | 598 | 565 | 552 |
| Coal (with $SO_2$ control) | 545 | 510 | 485 | 467 | 459 |
| Oil (with $SO_2$ control) | 494 | 461 | 438 | 421 | 413 |
| Oil (no $SO_2$ control) | 420 | 392 | 372 | 358 | 352 |

*Source*: U.S. Atomic Energy Commission, Division of Reactor Research and Development, *Power Plant Capital Costs: Current Trends and Sensitivity to Economic Parameters* (Washington: U.S. Government Printing Office, 1974), p. 43.

Cost per kilowatt is highest for smaller units of each type of plant and decreases as unit size is expanded. It should be noted, however, that as unit sizes increase, capital costs do not decline proportionately for nuclear, coal, and oil-fired units. For example, the estimate for a two-600-megawatt unit nuclear plant is approximately 29 percent higher than for a coal-fired plant of similar size. At the higher end of the scale, a two-1,300-megawatt unit nuclear plant is only about 20 percent more costly than the same sized coal plant. Put another way, the cost per kilowatt of capacity of a pressurized-water reactor plant declines by over 21 percent when unit size is increased from 600 to 1,300 megawatts, while the same increase in the size of a coal-fired plant results in a saving of less than 16 percent. Economies of scale are not the same for all types of plants.

In the area of power plant capital costs, the largest increases were in interest during construction and escalation during construction. These factors were interrelated in that higher levels of inflation put pressure on long-term interest rates. Both, in turn, were severely affected by longer plant construction schedules due to the increasing complexity of plant construction permit and licensing stages.[12] While large plant completion times were being estimated at around five years for projects beginning in the mid-1960s, plants under consideration in 1974 were subject to delay estimates of nearly ten years between project starts and commercial operation.

Although time-related costs have become proportionately more important in the capital costs of power plant construction, direct costs have become proportionately smaller. This has been due primarily to relatively small increases in the expense of turbine generators and nuclear steam supply systems. Estimates of the direct-cost components, craft labor and construction material and equipment, remained at approximately the same proportion of total cost for plants completed in 1973, as compared to those which will come on-stream in 1981.[13] Estimates of indirect power plant capital costs, including professional services, construction tools and material, and contingency expenses, increased at a slightly more rapid rate than aggregate power plant expenditures. Summaries of the various estimates for nuclear and coal-fired plants are illustrated in Figures 3.2 and 3.3 respectively.

## Transmission and Distribution

Expenditures on transmission and distribution facilities, while increasing in absolute amount, have consistently declined as a portion of total capital spending. From allocating nearly 58 percent of total capital expenditures on transmission and distribution in 1964, electric utilities had decreased this to only 34 percent a decade later. Although price increases for labor, land, materials, and capital were factors tending to escalate costs in this segment, technological improvements and increasing load densities helped to offset these effects. In addition, economies of scale were increasingly important.

# FIGURE 3.2

## Comparison of Nuclear Plant
## Total Cost Estimates for 1,000 Megawatt Units
### (millions of dollars)

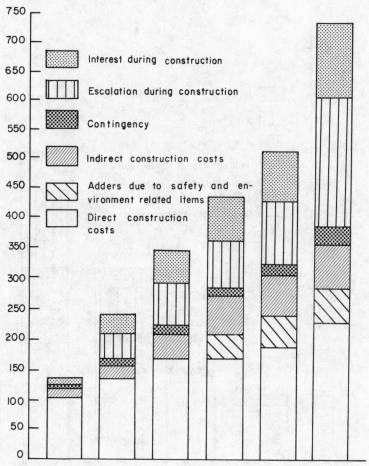

| | | | | | | |
|---|---|---|---|---|---|---|
| Experience | : | Mar. 1967 | Jun. 1969 | Jan. 1971 | Jan. 1973 | Jan. 1973 | Jan. 1973 |
| Start-of-project | : | Mar. 1967 | Jun. 1969 | Jan. 1971 | Jan. 1971 | Jan. 1973 | mid-1974 |
| Commercial operation | : | late-1972 | mid-1975 | Jan. 1978 | Jan. 1978 | Jan. 1981 | Jan. 1983 |

Source: U.S. Atomic Energy Commission, Division of Reactor Research and Development, *Power Plant Capital Costs: Current Trends and Sensitivity to Economic Parameters* (Washington: U.S. Government Printing Office, 1974), p. 3.

# FIGURE 3.3

## Comparison of Coal-Fired Plant
## Total Cost Estimates for 1,000 Megawatt Units
### (millions of dollars)

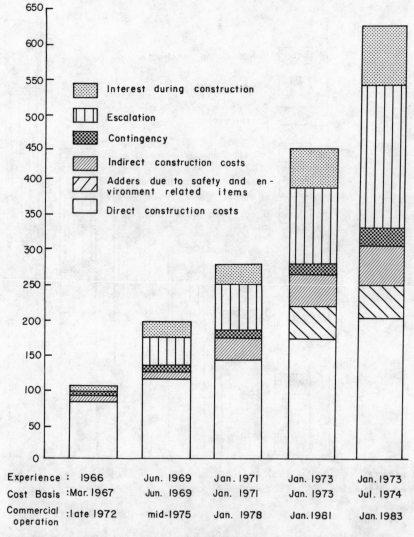

*Source*: U.S. Atomic Energy Commission, Division of Reactor Research and Development. *Power Plant Capital Costs: Current Trends and Sensitivity to Economic Parameters* (Washington: U.S. Government Printing Office, 1974), p. 10.

*Environmental Costs*

The electric utility industry spends a greater amount of money on anti-pollution equipment than any industry in the United States. Estimates by the McGraw-Hill Department of Economics projected that the industry would invest over $1.5 billion on air and water pollution controls in 1975 as compared to $8.4 billion for all of business, and approximately $4.6 billion for all manufacturing industries. Actual expenditures in 1974 were approximately $1.3 billion, $6.9 billion, and $4.0 billion, respectively. By 1977, McGraw-Hill estimates planned utility spending on air and water antipollution equipment at over $3.0 billion, or 31 percent of the combined expenditures of all businesses on similar investments.[14]

In addition to the capital costs of installing abatement facilities, which account for slightly less than 10 percent of the industry's capital expenditures, electric utilities have substantial operating costs and reliability problems associated with previously installed equipment. For example, forced-air water cooling towers must use a portion of a plant's electrical output to power fans that blow cooling air through the center section of the structure. One estimate is that this method of arresting thermal pollution consumes up to 3 percent of a plant's electrical output.[15] The cost of operating a dry-water cooling tower is even more expensive in terms of reduced electrical output.[16] In addition, the control of particulate emissions results in solid waste which must be disposed of.

The increase in costs of nuclear plants associated with the tightening of environmental restrictions has been significant. Table 3.4 shows that, in constant 1971 dollars, an estimated $12 million increase occurred for light-water reactor plants from 1971 to 1973, due to increased environmental standards. The changes were designed to help offset a number of environmental concerns including thermal pollution, noise pollution, and radioactive releases. If the list had been adjusted for inflation, interest charges, and indirect costs, the expense would be approximately twice that shown.

While capital and operating costs of environmental equipment take the major share of dollars, utilities also spend money on research in the area of pollution abatement. Typically, this area has suffered in recent years, partially because most electric utilities have been hard pressed to meet normal expenses, let alone find additional funds for research and development. It was estimated in 1971 that all research and development expenses—including those on pollution control—both by the utility industry and the equipment manufacturers, amounted to only about 0.2 percent of revenues or $150 million per year.[17] A more recent environmental research agenda of the Federal Power Commission envisions an increasing amount of funding devoted to this area. Table 3.5 shows the expected funding requirements of various environmental programs with respect to electric utilities, and Table 3.6 projects the funding responsibility of the programs. Total spending over the 1976-90 period will amount to over $10.5

TABLE 3.4

Light-Water Reactor Cost Increases Caused by Environmental
Changes between 1971 and 1973
(thousands of 1971 dollars)

| Change | Labor | Equipment and Materials |
|---|---|---|
| Turbine room | 250 | 150 |
| Water-intake structure | 2,631 | 1,266 |
| Radioactive release restrictions | 1,080 | 2,411 |
| Circulating water system | 961 | 1,367 |
| Condenser | 178 | 1,447 |
| Noise abatement | 218 | 145 |
| Total | 5,318 | 6,786 |

*Source*: U.S. Atomic Energy Commission, division of Reactor Research and Development, *Power Plant Capital Costs: Current Trends and Sensitivity to Economic Parameters* (Washington: U.S. Government Printing Office, 1974), p. 13.

billion, of which the utilities are expected to contribute less than $3 billion. Even if these estimates are only approximate, spending in the area of environmental research and development will result in increased cost to the industry.

A category closely related to environmental expense is the additional cost imposed by safety-related items. For nuclear facilities these include protection against site-related occurrences such as floods and earthquakes, and additional safeguards against loss-of-coolant accidents. It has been estimated that between 1971 and 1973, changes in safety-related items added nearly $22 million (in terms of 1971 dollars) to the cost of a 1,000-megawatt nuclear plant.[18]

## Fuel Costs

The skyrocketing cost of fossil fuels was the most significant factor in driving up the price of electricity to consumers during the early and mid-1970s. In part, this was due to the ability of the utilities to pass on higher fuel costs through fuel adjustment clauses that entailed no regulatory lag. Mostly, however, it was because the cost of coal, gas, and especially oil, increased by such large proportions. After remaining relatively constant in price throughout the 1960s, fossil-fuel costs began a rise in 1970 that gained momentum with each passing year. Cost increases over the decade 1964-74 amounted to 190 percent for coal, 89 percent for gas, and 488 percent for oil. While oil had traditionally

## TABLE 3.5

### Environmental Research Agenda Funding Requirements
(millions of dollars)

| Environmental Program | 1976 | 1977 | 1978 | 1979 | 1980 | 1981-85 | 1986-90 |
|---|---|---|---|---|---|---|---|
| Effects research | | | | | | | |
| Health | 130 | 134 | 172 | 194 | 215 | 795 | 850 |
| Ecological | 107 | 123 | 147 | 164 | 175 | 740 | 750 |
| Welfare | 23 | 28 | 32 | 37 | 40 | 115 | 115 |
| Instrumentation and monitoring | 43 | 41 | 38 | 36 | 35 | 155 | 155 |
| Environmental processes | 31 | 31 | 31 | 31 | 31 | 180 | 175 |
| Control technology | | | | | | | |
| Fossil fuel | 138 | 154 | 165 | 167 | 168 | 237 | 210 |
| Nuclear | 185 | 255 | 267 | 258 | 269 | 769 | 730 |
| Unconventional | 10 | 11 | 16 | 16 | 13 | 65 | 20 |
| Implementation research | 15 | 17 | 20 | 22 | 25 | 125 | 150 |
| Total | 682 | 794 | 880 | 925 | 971 | 3,181 | 3,155 |

*Source:* Adapted from U.S. Federal Power Commission, *Task Force Report: Environmental Research* (Washington: U.S. Government Printing Office, 1974), p. I-22.

49

## TABLE 3.6

### Environmental Research Agenda Funding Responsibility
### (percent of total funding)

| Environmental Program | Government | Industry |
|---|---|---|
| Effects research | | |
|    Health | 90 | 10 |
|    Ecological | 80 | 20 |
|    Welfare | 50 | 50 |
| Instrumentation and monitoring | 85 | 15 |
| Environmental processes | 80 | 20 |
| Control technology | | |
|    Basic research | 90 | 10 |
|    Applied research | 75 | 25 |
|    Applied development | 25 | 75 |
|    Engineering development | 15 | 85 |
| Implementation research | 75 | 25 |

Source: U.S. Federal Power Commission, *Task Force Report: Environmental Research* (Washington: U.S. Government Printing Office, 1974), p. I-23.

been the most expensive fuel burned, the cost per million Btu remained fairly competitive between the different fossil fuels until 1970. The regulated price of interstate gas and long-term contracts for coal kept price increases for these fuels below that for oil (see Table 3.7).

As a result of the various proportional changes in cost for the different fuels, not all companies were affected to the same degree. Utilities in Florida and the Northeast were hit the hardest, since they were most dependent upon foreign oil. Some companies in the West—those with large amounts of hydro capacity—were virtually unaffected except insofar as they continued to add fossil-fuel plants to supplement capacity. Electric utilities in the Midwest and Southwest, which burned coal and gas, experienced large cost increases, but even those were moderate compared to oil-burning systems. Overall, the distribution of total electric utility revenues required to pay for fuel increased from 19.8 percent in 1970, to 24.3 percent in 1973, to 34.8 percent in 1974.[19]

Although uranium fuel prices increased rapidly in 1974 and 1975, the expense for this fuel remains a small portion of nuclear power plant generating costs compared to fuel costs for fossil-fuel plants.[20] It has been estimated that a five-fold increase in the price of uranium would be approximately equivalent to a $2 per barrel rise in the cost of oil.[21] The Atomic Energy Commission projected the generation costs displayed in Table 3.8 for 1,000-megawatt light-water reactor plants and coal-burning plants coming on-stream in 1982. It should be

TABLE 3.7

Cost of Fossil Fuels for Electricity Generation, 1962-74
(cents per million Btu consumed)

| Fuel Type | Year | | | | | | | | | | | | |
|---|---|---|---|---|---|---|---|---|---|---|---|---|---|
| | 1962 | 1963 | 1964 | 1965 | 1966 | 1967 | 1968 | 1969 | 1970 | 1971 | 1972 | 1973 | 1974 |
| Coal | 25.6 | 25.0 | 24.5 | 24.4 | 24.7 | 25.2 | 25.5 | 26.6 | 31.1 | 36.0 | 38.1 | 41.9 | 71.0 |
| Gas | 26.4 | 25.5 | 25.4 | 25.0 | 25.0 | 24.7 | 25.1 | 25.4 | 27.0 | 28.0 | 30.3 | 35.2 | 48.1 |
| Oil | 34.5 | 33.5 | 32.7 | 33.1 | 32.4 | 32.2 | 32.8 | 31.9 | 36.6 | 51.5 | 58.8 | 78.3 | 192.2 |
| Weighted average | 26.5 | 25.8 | 25.3 | 25.3 | 25.4 | 25.7 | 26.1 | 26.9 | 30.7 | 36.4 | 39.9 | 48.4 | 90.9 |

*Sources*: U.S. Federal Power Commission, *Steam Electric Plant Construction Cost and Annual Production Expenses* (Washington: U.S. Government Printing Office, 1974), p. XVII; and Standard and Poor's *Industry Surveys: Utilities-Electric* (New York: Standard and Poor, 1975), p. U-17.

## TABLE 3.8

### Estimated Generating Costs for 1,000 Megawatt Plants, Including Escalation to 1982
#### (mills per kilowatt hour)

| Cost Component | Light-Water Reactor | Coal |
|---|---|---|
| Capital | 15.5 | 13.0 |
| Fuel | 5.6 | 12.2 |
| Operating and maintenance | 1.5 | 3.7 |
| Total | 22.6 | 28.9 |

*Source*: U.S. Atomic Energy Commission, *The Nuclear Industry, 1974* (Washington: U.S. Government Printing Office, 1975), p. 20.

remembered, however, that the Atomic Energy Commission has consistently underestimated the increase in capital costs, which play such a major role in determining the cost of power from nuclear plants.

## NOTES

1. U.S. Federal Power Commission, *Statistics of Privately Owned Electric Utilities in the United States, 1972* (Washington: U.S. Government Printing Office, 1974), p. VIII.

2. ———, *Typical Electric Bills, 1974* (Washington: U.S. Government Printing Office, 1974), pp. XI, XVIII, and XXIII.

3. See Edward Berlin, Charles Cicchetti, and William Gillen, *Perspective on Power* (Cambridge, Mass.: Ballinger Publishing Co., 1974), pp. 16-23.

4. David L. Scott. *Pollution in the Electric Power Industry* (Lexington, Mass.: D. C. Heath and Co., 1973), Chapter 4.

5. Martin T. Farris, *Public Utilities* (Boston: Houghton Mifflin Co., 1973), pp. 291-92.

6. Murray L. Weidenbaum, *Financing the Electric Utility Industry* (New York: Edison Electric Institute, 1974), p. 48.

7. See P. O. Steiner, "Peak Loads and Efficient Pricing," *Quarterly Journal of Economics* 71, no. 4 (November 1957): 585-610.

8. Berlin, op. cit., p. 25.

9. The *Wall Street Journal*, April 1, 1975, p. 38.

10. United Engineers and Constructors, Inc., *Current Status and Future Technical and Economic Potential of Light Water Reactors*, U.S. Atomic Energy Commission Report WASH-1082 (Washington: U.S. Government Printing Office, 1968).

11. ———, *1000 MWE Central Station Power Plant Investment Cost Study*, U.S. Atomic Energy Commission Report WASH-1230 (Washington: U.S. Government Printing Office, 1972).

12. U.S. Atomic Energy Commission, Division of Reactor Research and Development, *Power Plant Capital Costs: Current Trends and Sensitivity to Economic Parameters* (Washington: U.S. Government Printing Office, 1974), p. 9.

13. Ibid., p. 5.

14. McGraw-Hill Economics Department, "8th Annual McGraw-Hill Survey: Pollution Control Expenditures," May 16, 1975, p. 10.

15. *SFI Bulletin No. 191* (January-February 1968), reprinted in U.S. Congress, Senate, Subcommittee on Air and Water Pollution, *Hearing on Thermal Pollution—1968,* 90th Cong., 2nd Sess., 1968, p. 84.

16. Statement of Harry Perry, Research Advisor to Assistant Secretary for Mineral Resources, U.S. Congress, Joint Committee on Atomic Energy, *Hearings on Environmental Effects of Producing Electric Power,* 91st Cong., 2nd Sess., 1969, p. 336.

17. Statement of Edward E. David, Director, Office of Science and Technology, U.S. Congress, House, Subcommittee on Communications and Power, *Hearings on Powerplant Siting and Environmental Protection,* 92nd Cong., 1st Sess., 1971, p. 295.

18. U.S. Atomic Energy Commission, op. cit., p. 14-15.

19. "1975 Annual Statistical Report," *Electrical World* 183, no. 6 (March 15, 1975): 69.

20. See The *Wall Street Journal,* September 9, 1975, p. 7.

21. Statement of Thomas B. Cochran, Staff Physicist for the Natural Resource Defense Council, U.S. Congress, House, Committee on Interior and Insular Affairs, Subcommittee on Energy and the Environment, *Oversight Hearings on Nuclear Energy—Overview of the Major Issues,* 94th Cong., 1st Sess., 1975, p. 649.

In financing the expansion of capital assets during the era previously discussed, electric utilities became a major factor in the capital markets. From capital spending of $3 billion in 1948, the industry increased its outlays to over $20 billion in 1974.[1] Funds raised externally through debt and equity sales increased at an even more rapid rate during this period and investors began looking at many of the securities with growing skepticism. The investor-owned segment of the utilities required the vast majority of funds, and its share of the industry's total capital expenditures increased from approximately 70 percent in 1955 to 81 percent in 1970.[2] While the increased penetration appeared to have peaked in the early 1970s, this trend could again begin increasing as investor-owned companies generate power to be purchased and resold to consumers by the nonprivate systems. The result would be a decreasing proportion of electric sales but a continually increasing share of capital expenditures by investor-owned systems. However, should the industry follow the lead of Consolidated Edison in selling generating plants to public power authorities, the trend could be reversed.[3]

Since the investor-owned companies raise capital under decidedly different circumstances than cooperative, federal, and municipal systems, these various alternatives to private ownership will be analyzed in separate sections.

## INVESTOR-OWNED SYSTEMS

Investor-owned electric systems raise long-term funds both externally with issues of common stock, preferred stock, and debt, and internally through retained earnings, depreciation, and deferred taxes. As with most private businesses, external funding is primarily used when depreciation and retained earnings (deferred taxes provide only a small proportion of total requirements) prove insufficient for capital outlays. The capital markets, therefore, are treated as analogous to a "court of last resort" to be used when firms are not able to generate needed funds internally.

Whereas additional net investment spending and the resulting use of the capital markets by unregulated companies indicate the presence of potentially profitable investment opportunities, the same is not necessarily true for electric power companies. This is so because public utilities are expected to supply adequate amounts of their product even though the prospects for earnings might not be sufficiently encouraging to justify additional capital spending. Another related problem occurs due to the necessity of having increased generation, transmission, and distribution facilities available when needed. Because of this, the industry has only very limited discretion in timing its placements of debt and equity issues in an attempt to minimize the cost of capital. The result has been large amounts of debt sold at historically high interest rates and new equity issued at big discounts from book value.

## Internal Sources of Funds

Depreciation can increase only gradually over short periods of time for any type of company, and since the contribution of retained earnings for utilities is limited by dividend policy and a ceiling on rates of return, the electric power industry can, at best, count on relatively slow and steady increases in the generation of internal funds. Hence, during periods of quickening capital expenditures, depreciation, and retained earnings have provided a smaller proportion of total long-term needs.

As illustrated in Figure 4.1, investor-owned electric power companies were able to internally generate an increasing portion of total funds until 1962, when nearly 60 percent of all sources were provided by depreciation and amortization, deferred taxes, and retained earnings. During this period capital expenditures were relatively stable between $3 billion and $4 billion annually. Between 1958 and 1962, when these expenditures actually declined, internal funding jumped from 40 percent to 60 percent of aggregate needs. Throughout the late 1960s, as investment spending began to rise at a rapid pace, the utilities found it necessary to rely more heavily upon the capital markets as the proportion of internally generated funds began deteriorating. From a high of 60 percent of total funds in 1962, the contribution of this segment of financing declined to less than 30 percent in the early 1970s. This was the case even though internal funds increased in absolute amount from nearly $2 billion in 1962, to slightly less than $4.3 billion in 1972. During the same span, however, annual issues of debt and common and preferred stock rose from $1.4 billion to $9.7 billion.

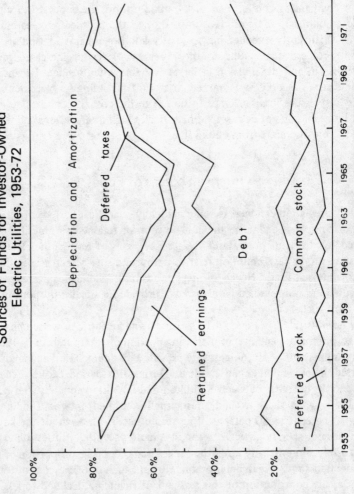

FIGURE 4.1

Sources of Funds for Investor-Owned
Electric Utilities, 1953-72

*Source*: U.S. Federal Power Commission, *Statistics of Privately Owned Electric Utilities in the United States* (Washington: U.S. Government Printing Office, various years).

*Depreciation*

A main goal of allowing depreciation as an expense is to let a business maintain original values of its fixed assets within the company. This is accomplished by changing a fixed asset into a current asset through the creation of an expense on the income statement that requires no cash outlay on the part of the company. The expense thus becomes a source of funds and can be used to replace the depleted capital stock at some future date.

Due to the capital intensive nature of the industry, depreciation is especially important to the electric utilities, and has been the largest source of internal funding. Over the last decade, however, this variable experienced the greatest decline of all sources in relative importance even though it increased in absolute amount in every year. While depreciation supplied over 41 percent of total funds in 1962, its contribution had declined to slightly under 21 percent by 1972. This erosion took place at the same time the dollar amount of depreciation more than doubled from $1.4 billion to $2.9 billion. The decreasing proportion of funds supplied by this source is not surprising in view of the rapid rise in capital requirements illustrated in Figure 4.2.

In the decade prior to 1963, capital outlays were relatively constant as economies of scale and technological improvements combined to offset a moderate rate of inflation.[4] During this period investor-owned electric utilities were able to generate increasing amounts of funds internally—especially through larger depreciation allowances as the asset base increased. However, subsequent expenditures increased very rapidly, and by 1972 capital outlays were being made at nearly four times the 1962 rate. Since funds generated by depreciation are partially determined by existing assets subject to the depreciation charge, and since additions to the capital stock in any single year do not significantly affect the aggregate amount of these assets, this source provided a smaller percentage of total funds as investment spending began its rapid climb. The other factor determing the contribution of this source, the average rate of depreciation, changed only slightly over the past 25 years (see Table 4.1).

As net additions to the capital stock were made to meet the rising demand for electricity and to satisfy increasingly tougher environmental standards, and as inflationary pressures required the acquisition of new assets at prices significantly higher than those being replaced, the discrepancy between actual expenditures and depreciation allowances widened.

*Retained Earnings*

Retained earnings—the portion of earnings reinvested in the industry rather than paid out as dividends to stockholders—is the other major internal

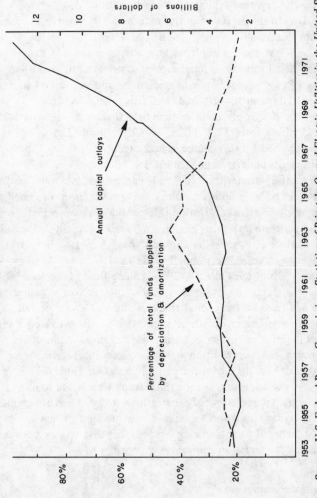

FIGURE 4.2

Capital Outlays and Percentage of Funds Supplied by
Depreciation and Amortization for Investor-Owned
Electric Utilities, 1953-72

*Source*: U.S. Federal Power Commission, *Statistics of Privately Owned Electric Utilities in the United States*
(Washington: U.S. Government Printing Office, various years).

### TABLE 4.1

### Average Rates of Depreciation for Investor-Owned Electric Utilities, 1948-66
(percent)

| Depreciated Asset | 1948 | 1951 | 1958 | 1961 | 1966 |
|---|---|---|---|---|---|
| Production | | | | | |
|   Steam | 2.5 | 2.5 | 2.5 | 2.7 | 2.8 |
|   Hydraulic | 1.3 | 1.4 | 1.2 | 1.5 | 1.6 |
|   Other | 3.7 | 3.7 | 3.8 | 3.3 | 3.7 |
| Transmission | 2.5 | 2.5 | 2.3 | 2.4 | 2.4 |
| Distribution | 2.8 | 2.8 | 2.9 | 2.8 | 3.1 |
| General | 3.6 | 4.4 | 4.6 | 4.3 | 3.7 |
|   Composite | 2.5 | 2.6 | 2.6 | 2.7 | 2.8 |

*Source*: U.S. Federal Power Commission, *Electric Utility Depreciation Practices* (Washington, D.C.: U.S. Government Printing Office, 1968).

funding source. This component is important not only for the dollars it contributes toward capital spending, but also because earnings have such a great effect upon the ability of the industry to raise funds externally. When earnings are relatively high, of good quality, and exhibit a positive trend, debt and preferred stock can be sold with lower yields and common stock can generally be issued at a higher price-earnings ratio. The latter is of special significance since higher earnings supporting a higher price-earnings ratio allow companies to issue a smaller number of shares to raise a given amount of funds.

Retained earnings have been far less stable than depreciation on both an absolute and a proportional basis, and in 1972 supplied only $1,166 million as against $2,896 million for the latter. The relative contribution of retained earnings was much greater during the 1960s, when it averaged nearly 11 percent of total sources, than it was in either the 1950s or the early 1970s. One of the major reasons underlying this decade of relative prosperity was the ability of the utilities to generate electricity at lower cost and, in turn, pass a portion of these savings on to consumers in a lower product price. From 1960 to 1969, the average revenue per residential kilowatt-hour of electricity sold fell from 2.47¢ to 2.09¢.[5] With regulatory lag operating in their favor, the utilities were able to increase their return on common stock equity from 11.3 percent to 12.2 percent during this period.[6] Fewer critics of the industry existed in an era of declining prices for electric power, and it was therefore easier for the utilities to earn a higher rate of return. However, when electric costs started to rise in 1970, the rates of return obtained during the previous decade became more difficult to achieve, especially since regulatory agencies had become accustomed to lowering rates. Long lags between requests for and implementation of rate increases became the rule as utilities immediately filed for new increases after partial relief had been granted. While 59 electric rate cases were pending at the end of 1970, 175 were being considered in early 1975. The amount involved in these cases had increased from $512 million to $4 billion, respectively.[7] The increasing costs were brought about by a number of factors over which the industry had little or no control including higher interest rates and construction expenses, increased fuel costs, and pollution abatement outlays, all of which were not offset by improved economies.[8]

Another factor affecting retained earnings as a source of funds is the dividend payout ratio displayed in Figure 4.3. A survey of electric utility companies included in the Dow Jones Utility Average shows that during the 1953-62 period, when internal sources of funds increased their relative contribution to

## FIGURE 4.3

### Capital Requirements Supplied by Internal Sources and Dividend Payout Ratios for Investor-Owned Electric Utilities, 1953-72

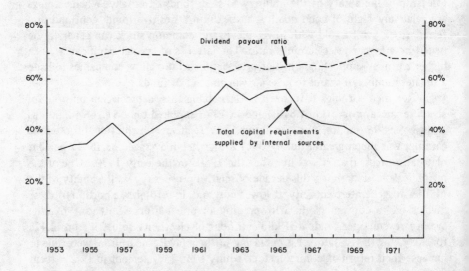

Source: U.S. Federal Power Commission, *Statistics of Privately Owned Electric Utilities in the United States* (Washington: U.S. Government Printing Office, various years).

capital expenditures, the common stock cash dividend payout ratio declined from 72 percent to 61 percent of earnings after taxes.* However, from 1962 until 1972 the ratio increased from 61 percent back to near its former high level. Since electric utilities, as well as most other companies, typically increase dividends only gradually during periods of rising net income, the resulting lower payout ratio tends to accentuate the rising proportion of funds available from retained earnings. Conversely, during periods of falling return on owners' equity, dividends remain the same or are even increased resulting in a higher payout ratio and a smaller proportional contribution from retained earnings.

## Deferred Taxes

Deferred taxes provided diminishing help to the industry. After contributing from 5.9 percent to 7.4 percent of total funds during the latter half of the 1950s, this source declined to approximately 1 percent annually from 1964 through 1970 and 1.6 percent in 1971 and 1972. Deferred taxes originate from the ability of electric utilities to amortize the cost of certain assets less rapidly for financial accounting purposes than for income tax purposes. Over a 20-year period this has included the 3 percent investment tax credit, the 4 percent job development tax credit, the asset depreciation range system, the "Guideline Lives," and liberalized depreciation and accelerated amortization.[9] The effect of these various credits and income tax deductions is to postpone or permanently reduce income taxes. This deferment is perhaps most easily seen in the practice of recording accelerated depreciation for income tax purposes but using straight-line depreciation for book purposes. Since the former method generates larger expenses than the latter in the early life of an asset, income reported to the government and taxes to be paid on this income are postponed until later years. In many cases, however, the net result was a flow through of the tax reduction to consumers in the form of lower electric rates rather than significant benefits for the utilities.[10]

---

*The survey includes American Electric Power, Cleveland Electric Illuminating, Commonwealth Edison, Consolidated Edison, Detroit Edison, Houston Light and Power, Pacific Gas and Electric, Philadelphia Electric, Public Service Electric and Gas, and Southern California Edison.

## External Sources of Funds

While the typical nonfinancial corporation secures only one-fourth to one-third of its total long-term funding requirements from outside sources, investor-owned electric utilities have generally been forced to raise on the order of 50 to 60 percent of funds externally. In the most recent years this proportion has been even greater. Debt and preferred stock have traditionally occupied a larger position in the capital structures of electric utilities than in the financing of companies in other industries. This high degree of leverage has generally been justified by a stability of income and the resulting ability to meet fixed expenses with minimum risk. The ability of investor-owned utilities to meet these fixed expenses has been challenged in a recent study. Although this study concentrated primarily on the financial impact of pollution abatement expenditures (which, as noted, have a considerable impact on the utility industry), the conclusion was reached that the debt capacity of investor-owned electric utilities has declined in recent years.[11]

External funding—debt, common stock, and preferred stock—became increasingly relied upon in the 1960s after declining in relative usage from 1953 to 1962. After supplying nearly 71 percent of total funds in 1951, external sources dropped to 41 percent in 1962 before increasing again so that over 71 percent of total financing requirements were supplied by outside sources. Since external funds are treated as a residual component in that outside sources are tapped when internally generated funds prove inadequate to provide sufficient financing, it was necessary for investor-owned electric utilities to increasingly employ the financial markets when capital expenditures began to rise at a rapid rate. This was particularly evident in debt issues and somewhat more sporadic in the distribution of equities.

The trend in sources of external financing is more obvious upon examination of the changing capital structure of Class A and B investor-owned electric utilities shown in Table 4.2. Until the early 1970s debt had shown a steady increase in importance at the expense of preferred stock and, to a lesser extent, common equity. Beginning in 1971, however, large increases in preferred stock issues more than offset the continuing decline of common equity, so that the trend to a greater percentage of debt in capital structures was at least temporarily reversed. It should be kept in mind that common equity includes not only new common stock issues, but also additions to retained earnings—the latter being an internal source of funds.

*Debt*

Debt became increasingly important in electric utility financing during the 1960s. From 1953 until 1960, annual net bond issues generally remained in the

## TABLE 4.2

### Capital Structure of Investor-Owned Electric Utilities, 1950-72
### (percent)

| Year | Long-Term Debt | Preferred Stock | Common Equity |
|------|---------------|-----------------|---------------|
| 1950 | 48.9 | 13.7 | 37.4 |
| 1951 | 49.2 | 13.5 | 37.3 |
| 1952 | 48.7 | 13.0 | 38.3 |
| 1953 | 49.8 | 12.3 | 37.4 |
| 1954 | 50.4 | 12.4 | 37.2 |
| 1955 | 50.7 | 12.3 | 37.0 |
| 1956 | 51.1 | 12.4 | 36.5 |
| 1957 | 52.4 | 11.6 | 36.0 |
| 1958 | 52.8 | 11.4 | 35.8 |
| 1959 | 52.8 | 11.0 | 36.2 |
| 1960 | 52.8 | 10.7 | 36.5 |
| 1961 | 52.8 | 10.4 | 36.8 |
| 1962 | 52.4 | 10.3 | 37.3 |
| 1963 | 52.1 | 10.0 | 37.9 |
| 1964 | 51.8 | 9.6 | 38.6 |
| 1965 | 51.5 | 9.5 | 39.0 |
| 1966 | 52.3 | 9.5 | 38.2 |
| 1967 | 53.0 | 9.6 | 37.4 |
| 1968 | 53.8 | 9.6 | 36.6 |
| 1969 | 54.6 | 9.4 | 36.1 |
| 1970 | 54.8 | 9.8 | 35.4 |
| 1971 | 54.2 | 10.7 | 35.1 |
| 1972 | 53.1 | 11.8 | 35.1 |

*Source*: U.S. Federal Power Commission, *Statistics of Privately Owned Electric Utilities in the United States* (Washington: U.S. Government Printing Office, various years).

$1 billion to $1.5 billion range, and in the early 1960s new issues actually declined to under $1 billion per year. But subsequent years showed increasing use of debt. By the early 1970s, new issues had risen steadily to slightly less than $5 billion annually. The increasing reliance upon debt was even more startling when compared to other sources of funds. As a percentage of all sources, debt declined to a low of approximately 23 percent in 1962 and then rapidly climbed back to about 44 percent during the late 1960s. It should be noted, however, that this large amount of debt as a portion of new financing was not inconsistent with funding operations during the late 1940s and the 1950s.

One big difference in financing through the use of long-term borrowing during these two periods was the marked change in interest rates necessary to place the debt. As displayed in Figure 4.4 the interest rate for utility bonds increased from approximately 3.5 percent in 1953 to around 8 percent in the early 1970s. As older, low-interest bonds were turned over with higher-interest securities and additional high-interest debt was issued, interest coverage ratios deteriorated even though debt as a portion of all new financing was not out of line with earlier periods. The resulting rapid increase of embedded interest cost and decline of interest coverage during recent years is clearly shown in Table 4.3. One study of the prospect-uses of utilities planning to issue long-term debt in late 1973 and 1974 showed that approximately two dozen had ratios of 2.3 or less.[12]

## FIGURE 4.4

### Interest Rates for Utility Debt and Net Debt Issues by Investor-Owned Electric Utilities, 1953-72

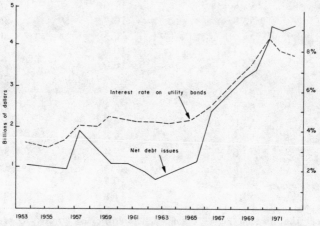

*Sources:* U.S. Federal Power Commission, *Statistics of Privately Owned Electric Utilities in the United States* (Washington: U.S. Government Printing Office, various years); and Board of Governors of the Federal Reserve System, *Federal Reserve Bulletin* (Washington: U.S. Government Printing Office, various years).

There are a number of injurious consequences which have resulted from declining coverage ratios. Since this variable is one of the primary determinants in the rating of debt by major bond rating companies such as Moody's and Standard and Poor's, the downward trend has resulted in the downgrading of debt for many electric utilities. This was particularly evident in 1970 through 1973, when ratings of 50 electric utility bonds were downgraded and only five were upgraded.[13] The effect of the changes in ratings was that new issues of downgraded companies had to carry even higher interest coupons in order to compensate investors for the greater risk they perceived having to assume. In some cases

## TABLE 4.3

### Embedded Interest Cost and Interest Coverage for Investor-Owned Electric Utilities, 1965-72

| Year | Embedded Interest Cost (percent) | Interest Coverage before Income Taxes |
|------|----------------------------------|----------------------------------------|
| 1965 | 3.8 | 5.46 |
| 1966 | 3.9 | 5.33 |
| 1967 | 4.0 | 4.95 |
| 1968 | 4.3 | 4.61 |
| 1969 | 4.6 | 4.18 |
| 1970 | 5.1 | 3.50 |
| 1971 | 5.5 | 3.10 |
| 1972 | 5.7 | 2.98 |

*Source*: U.S. Federal Power Commission, *Statistics of Privately Owned Electric Utilities in the United States* (Washington: U.S. Government Printing Office, various years).

utilities were unable to place new issues with financial institutions because of the lower ratings. The most serious effect of falling interest coverage ratios was a limit on the legal ability of some utilities to issue new debt due to restrictive provisions in existing indenture agreements. Typically, earnings before interest and income taxes must cover interest charges at least twice before new debt can be issued.[14]

As interest rates increased and the term structure of these rates shifted, the industry began substituting increasing amounts of commercial paper and bank loans for longer-term commitments. Increasing reliance was also placed upon foreign short-term borrowing and one utility reportedly arranged $10 million in revolving credit with two European banks.[15] From the early 1960s, when short-term debt as a percentage of total debt approximated 2 percent, the ratio had increased to over 6 percent by the early 1970s.[16] While this method of financing was at times advantageous and prevented firms from being locked in to very high long-term interest rates, it also reduced the ability of the utilities to borrow for financial emergencies and supplied a limited amount of capital that needed to be refinanced frequently. Utilities had typically used short-term borrowings to provide funds through periods when permanent financing was not yet needed. It appears that a more recent trend, however, has been to substitute cheaper and more easily obtainable short-term funds in instances where long-term money would normally have been used, thereby violating the financial axiom that capital assets should be financed with long-term commitments.

One method of acquiring the use of a long-term asset without having to finance its purchase is leasing or "off-balance-sheet financing." With this type of acquisition, a third party—typically a bank or insurance company—purchases and finances an asset such as nuclear fuel, office equipment, or computer facilities, and leases it under long-term contract to a utility. Since the lessor is the owner of the asset, it retains the tax advantages of the investment tax credit, depreciation allowances, and interest deductions, and passes these on to the lessee, who might not be able to take advantage of them, in the form of lower lease payments. Although there has been much debate on the proper method of accounting for this type of obligation in a firm's financial statement, standard practice has not required it to be shown as a form of funded indebtedness. As such, the industry's interest coverage and debt ratios are overly optimistic since the lessee generally assumes the risks of ownership.

A recent innovation in debt financing and another type of "off-balance-sheet financing," is the use of industrial revenue bonds to provide funds for pollution control facilities. Congress enacted a ceiling on the size of a debt issue which could be used for industrial development, but specifically omitted bonds which were being used to finance pollution abatement equipment. These instruments are sold by public agencies, although the utility using the proceeds guarantees both principal and interest payments over the life of the bonds. Interest is exempt from federal income taxes and may also avoid state and local taxation depending on state and local tax codes. This exemption results in a lower coupon rate than that for comparable corporate bonds and also provides additional potential buyers of the debt, such as insurance companies and banks, which might not normally be interested in similar taxable securities. The money generated by these bonds has rapidly increased in recent years as evidenced by a rise in the amount of such issues from slightly under $127 million in all of 1972 to nearly $1.6 billion during the first nine months of 1975.[17]

### Preferred Stock

Although electric utilities continued to be the largest issuers of preferred stock, this source of funds consistently ranked behind debt and common equity in importance. After supplying approximately 7 percent of total requirements during the 1950s, preferred usage dropped rapidly in the early 1960s before recovering its historical position during the latter part of the decade. The decline in preferred stock issues occurred at a time when internal funds were supplying a large portion of financing needs and new common stock distributions were at record high levels. While these senior equity issues have the dual advantage of carrying no maturity date and no legal obligation to pay dividends except prior to those on common stock, their dividends are not deductible for income tax purposes. This puts preferred stock at a competitive disadvantage with debt, which pays tax deductible interest, and makes the former carry a significantly higher explicit cost of financing. In spite of this, investor-owned electric utilities virtually flooded the capital markets with preferred issues in the early 1970s as they attempted to strengthen their badly eroded equity bases. In the first three years of the 1970s alone, issues of senior equity issues totaled slightly over $5 billion, or more than had been sold in the previous 23 years.

### Common Stock

The remaining portion of external financing is supplied through the issuance of common stock. This source provided widely varying amounts of funds over the past three decades. For example, the $717 million which was raised in common equity sales in 1952 was not surpassed until 1963 when $732 million in common stock was sold. This, in turn, was a peak not reached again until 1969. In the early 1970s, electric utilities sold much larger amounts of common equity, and sales of $6,855 million in the first three years of the decade were equal to net issues over the previous 12-year period.

That this source of funds is treated as a residual by investor-owned companies is demonstrated by the fact that common equity in the aggregate capitalization of these firms did not rise above 39.0 percent or fall below 35.1 percent from 1937 to 1972. There was, however, a decline subsequent to 1965 when the maximum of 39.0 percent was reached. This deterioration in capitalization during the latter half of the 1960s appears to have occurred primarily because of a reluctance to issue common stock at what was then considered to be depressed prices. Figure 4.5 illustrates the pressure under which equity financing went during that span of time.

## FIGURE 4.5

### Measures of Performance for the Common Stock of Investor-Owned Electric Utilities, 1953-73

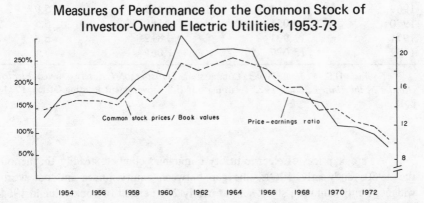

*Source*: Computed from data on electric utilities listed in Dow-Jones Utility Average.

Price-earnings ratios of investor-owned electric utilities fell steadily from a high of 22 in 1961 to slightly under 10 in 1973. This was the case even though reported earnings and dividends per share generally increased throughout the decade. There began to be serious doubt during the late 1960s and early 1970s, however, about the quality of reported earnings and the resulting ability to continue raising cash dividends. This was due in large part to the increasing portion of earnings represented by credits for expected future returns on construction in progress. Since plants under construction are not permitted in a utility's rate base, the allowance for funds used during construction represents a portion of construction expenses and is comprised of the cost of debt used for construction and a reasonable rate of return on equity capital. As an example of the importance of this type of income, American Electric Power, one of the companies used in calculating the data for Figure 4.5, reported an increase in earnings per share to $2.63 in 1972 from $2.00 in 1967, which included credits of $1.10 and $.16 per share respectively.[18] Consequently, exclusive of the credit, earnings per share actually declined from $1.84 to $1.53. The increasing magnitude of the allowance for funds used during construction is displayed in Table 4.4

## TABLE 4.4

### Allowance for Funds Used during Construction, 1968-72 (millions of dollars)

| Year | Average Construction Work in Progress | Allowance for Funds Used during Construction | Percent of Average Construction Work in Progress |
|------|---------------------------------------|----------------------------------------------|--------------------------------------------------|
| 1968 | 5,157 | 275 | 3.8 |
| 1969 | 6,814 | 403 | 5.9 |
| 1970 | 9,031 | 588 | 6.5 |
| 1971 | 11,931 | 812 | 6.8 |
| 1972 | 15,077 | 1,069 | 7.1 |

Source: U.S. Federal Power Commission, *Statistics of Privately Owned Electric Utilities in the United States, 1972* (Washington: U.S. Government Printing Office, 1974), p. IX.

As stock prices of electric utility companies climbed steadily throughout the 1950s and early 1960s, the gap between equity prices and net worth widened, until common stock sold at nearly 260 percent of book value in 1964. Once this peak was reached, however, the pressure on utility stock prices was such that, in the 1970s, many companies found their common equity selling at discounts from book value. The elimination of the premium was due not only to the decrease in stock prices, but also to the gradual increase in book values as net income not paid to shareholders in dividends was accumulating in retained earnings. It appears that utility managements believed the deterioration to be of a temporary nature during the early stages of the decline, and new placements of common stock from 1965 through 1968 were abnormally low. For example, the $287 million of common stock sold in 1966 had been surpassed in every year since 1947. During the same year, debt issues had doubled to $2.41 billion from $1.26 billion in 1965, and subsequent years saw even more borrowing to support growth and replacement spending. Unfortunately, the deteriorating trend in equity prices did not reverse itself, and it became necessary for the investor-owned electric utilities to issue more common and preferred stock beginning in 1970, in order to keep their capital bases from becoming overburdened with debt. The consequences of issuing this common stock at prices below book value seriously undermined future financing possibilities but the industry was left with little choice.[19]

## PUBLICLY AND COOPERATIVELY OWNED SYSTEMS

Three types of publicly and cooperatively owned systems generate and/or distribute electric power for consumers—municipal, federal, and rural electric cooperatives. While these three systems have numerical superiority over investor-owned systems of nearly 2,900 to 500 respectively, investor-owned systems are by far dominant in terms of capacity and sales.[20]

### Municipal Electric Utilities

Municipal utilities raise funds externally through the contributions of municipalities (similar to common stock issues of private companies) and by the placement of long-term debt. Internal funds are supplied by surplus from operations and by depreciation allowances.

In financing capital expenditures, municipal systems have typically relied less upon external sources than have investor-owned systems. Except in the mid-1950s and in the late 1960s and 1970s, when external funding supplied from 40 percent to 60 percent of aggregate requirements, debt and municipal investment usually provided significantly less than half of total funds (see Table 4.5). Of the two external sources, long-term debt was by far the most important. As the systems grew in size and capital expenditures expanded, municipal investment generally remained at between $10 million and $40 million annually (and in the years 1961, 1963, and 1972 was actually negative), while long-term debt

# TABLE 4.5

## Sources of Funds of Municipal Electric Utilities, 1950-72
### (millions of dollars)

| Year | Long-Term Debt | Municipal Investment | Percent External | Depreciation and Amortization | Surplus | Percent Internal |
|---|---|---|---|---|---|---|
| 1950 | 49.4 | 20.5 | 38.5 | 44.5 | 67.2 | 61.5 |
| 1951 | 99.6 | 10.8 | 48.9 | 48.9 | 67.9 | 51.4 |
| 1952 | 126.8 | 2.1 | 50.8 | 53.5 | 71.9 | 49.2 |
| 1953 | 26.6 | 11.4 | 18.8 | 58.1 | 106.5 | 81.2 |
| 1954 | 96.4 | 5.4 | 37.0 | 63.4 | 110.3 | 63.0 |
| 1955 | 59.8 | 14.3 | 31.9 | 71.7 | 86.4 | 68.1 |
| 1956 | 312.8 | 5.5 | 63.5 | 77.2 | 105.8 | 36.5 |
| 1957 | 255.8 | 22.8 | 57.4 | 83.8 | 122.6 | 42.6 |
| 1958 | 159.2 | 20.4 | 45.2 | 90.6 | 127.1 | 54.8 |
| 1959 | 327.4 | 1.5 | 58.6 | 100.5 | 132.0 | 41.4 |
| 1960 | 137.8 | 21.7 | 38.5 | 109.2 | 146.1 | 61.5 |
| 1961 | 161.6 | (11.2)a | 25.7 | 121.2 | 312.8 | 74.3 |
| 1962 | 420.8 | 8.3 | 44.9 | 145.3 | 382.2 | 55.1 |
| 1963 | 180.2 | ( 5.6)a | 29.0 | 156.5 | 271.2 | 71.0 |
| 1964 | 201.5 | 16.8 | 30.4 | 168.3 | 332.1 | 69.6 |
| 1965 | 179.6 | 44.4 | 37.5 | 178.8 | 194.3 | 62.5 |
| 1966 | 193.3 | 41.5 | 34.4 | 192.1 | 255.1 | 65.5 |
| 1967 | 465.8 | 32.8 | 49.5 | 205.4 | 303.2 | 50.5 |
| 1968 | 554.2 | 31.4 | 54.8 | 225.4 | 256.9 | 45.2 |
| 1969 | 323.2 | 13.3 | 40.1 | 238.8 | 263.4 | 59.9 |
| 1970 | 542.0 | 19.8 | 49.9 | 253.7 | 310.8 | 50.1 |
| 1971 | 638.5 | 202.0 | 57.7 | 280.4 | 335.0 | 42.3 |
| 1972 | 845.5 | (46.6)a | 52.6 | 300.5 | 420.5 | 47.4 |

aNegative figure.

*Note:* Excludes the Niagara and St. Lawrence projects of The Power Authority of the State of New York.

In 1961 a new annual report form was initiated which led to an increase in the number of municipal utilities filing reports with the Federal Power Commission. This resulted in a 10 percent coverage increase beginning in 1962.

*Source:* U.S. Federal Power Commission, *Statistics of Publicly Owned Electric Utilities in the United States, 1972* (Washington: U.S. Government Printing Office, 1973), pp. XVIII and XXII.

increased from less than $100 million per year during the early 1950s to nearly $850 million in 1972. Since municipalities are permitted to issue revenue bonds which pay interest that is exempt from federal income taxes, the debt carries a significantly lower cost than similar taxable obligations of investor-owned companies.[21] In addition, these bonds are generally not included in the legal debt limits of most municipalities.[22]

Compared to the components of external funding there was a relatively even distribution between the internal sources of depreciation and surplus. While the former provided fewer dollars in each year since 1950, it generally remained at 50 to 80 percent of the contribution by surplus. As was the case with investor-owned utilities, depreciation supplied a gradually increasing dollar amount of funds over the years as the asset base expanded through larger capital expenditures.

## Federally Owned Electric Utilities

The Tennessee Valley Authority (TVA) is the only federal agency engaged in the generation and distribution of electric power which is allowed to issue its own debt obligations in the capital markets.[23] In addition to this borrowing authority, which was initiated in 1959 with a maximum of $1.75 billion and increased in 1960 to $5 billion, TVA also received proprietary capital from the U.S. government through bond purchases, property transfers, and appropriations. As a part of the TVA Act, The Tennessee Valley Authority was required to repay a portion of the net appropriation and a return on the outstanding investment to the U.S. Treasury each year. The return on investment was determined by the amount of the unrepaid appropriation and on the average interest rate payable by the Treasury on its total marketable public obligations at the beginning of the fiscal year.[24] TVA bonds have generally enjoyed credit ratings superior to similar debt instruments issued by investor-owned systems, and even though the former are not guaranteed as to principal or interest by the U.S. government, the debt service does have priority over repayments to the Treasury.[25] In addition, the return on federal appropriations has been at significantly lower rates than the corresponding cost of equity capital for private utilities. The result is a considerably lower cost of funds for the TVA system than for investor-owned electric utilities, although the former increased very rapidly in the early 1970s.

The remaining agencies of the federal system—the Corps of Engineers, Bureau of Reclamation, Bonneville Power Administration, and Southwestern Power Administration—have relied solely upon congressional appropriations for funding and, therefore, have had to compete with alternative federal projects for scarce monies.

## Cooperatively Owned Electric Utilities

While initial funds for cooperatively owned electric utilities originated with member contributions, a large portion of subsequent long-term capital needs came from loans supplied by the Rural Electrification Administration. The REA was established as a lending agency of the cooperatives through legislative enactment of the Rural Electrification Act of 1936. The loans offered through this agency were subsidized with low interest rates and carried 35-year repayment periods. In addition to debt financing, these systems also generated funds through net margins and depreciation, although the relative contribution of each of the three sources varied considerably depending upon the type of cooperative.

Since 1962, generating and transmission cooperatives have raised the vast majority of their funds by debt. For example, during the 1963-69 period, this group of cooperatives borrowed nearly 75 percent of total capital requirements.[26] Of the remaining sources—depreciation and net margin—the former increased gradually as the asset base expanded and consistently outpaced net margin in importance. The latter source provided only a small amount of funds during the last two decades.

While debt has also been important in the financing of distribution cooperatives, it contributed less than either depreciation or net margin. These latter sources provided continually increasing amounts of funds, while REA borrowings were treated as a residual and varied greatly in use over the last two decades.

Subsequent to 1971, most cooperatively owned systems have been required to support Rural Electrification Administration loans with supplemental financing from nongovernmental sources. In order to provide a source of supplemental financing, the National Rural Utilities Cooperative Finance Corporation was established in 1970 with contributions from 785 rural electric cooperatives. This organization was designed to provide short, intermediate, and long-term loans, and in 1974 made an additional $700 million in funds available to REA borrowers.[27] While distribution cooperatives were required to obtain from 10 percent to 30 percent of borrowing needs from outside sources, generation and transmission systems needed to find nearly all debt funds through external lenders. Although these latter loans carried an REA guarantee, the additional cost in higher interest payments was significant in view of the subsidized REA rate which was previously available.

# NOTES

1. "1975 Annual Statistical Report," *Electrical World* 183, no. 6 (March 15, 1975): 47.

2. U.S. Federal Power Commission, *1970 National Power Survey*, (Washington: U.S. Government Printing Office, 1971), p. I-20-2.

3. The *Wall Street Journal*, October 23, 1974, p. 38.

4. U.S. Federal Power Commission, op. cit., p. I-20-4.

5. ———, *Typical Electric Bills*, (Washington: U.S. Government Printing Office, various years).

6. ———, *Statistics of Privately-Owned Electric Utilities in the United States, 1971* (Washington: U.S. Government Printing Office, 1973), p. 30.

7. The *Wall Street Journal*, January 28, 1975, p. 1.

8. For more complete information on pollution costs, see David L. Scott, *Pollution in the Electric Power Industry: Its Control and Costs* (Lexington, Massachusetts: D.C. Heath & Co., 1973).

9. U.S. Congress, Senate, Committee on Interior and Insular Affairs, *Electric Utility Policy Issues*, Senate Resolution 45, 93rd Cong., 2nd Sess., 1974, p. 87.

10. Ibid., p. 88.

11. Marvin E. Ray, *The Environmental Crisis and Corporate Debt Policy* (Lexington, Massachusetts: D.C. Heath & Co., 1974).

12. Herman G. Rosen, "Utility Financing Problems and National Energy Policy," *Public Utilities Fortnightly* 94, no. 6 (September 12, 1974): 21.

13. Murray L. Weidenbaum, *Financing the Electric Utility Industry* (New York: Edison Electric Institute, 1974), p. 113.

14. Ibid., p. 58.

15. "Can Utilities Get the Megabucks to Build All Those Megawatts?" *Electrical World* 181, no. 11 (June 1, 1974): 287.

16. U.S. Federal Power Commission, *Statistics of Privately-Owned Electric Utilities in the United States* (Washington: U.S. Government Printing Office, various years).

17. "Tax Exempt Anti-Pollution IDBs up 45% in 9 Months to $1.5 Billion," *The Money Manager* 4, no. 41 (October 14, 1975): 51.

18. Charles Tatham, "Interest During Construction and Price-Earnings Ratios," *Public Utilities Fortnightly* 92, no. 7 (September 27, 1973): 36.

19. Rosen, op. cit., pp. 22-23.

20. "Private, Public Power Coexist Peacefully," *Electrical World* 181, no. 11 (June 1, 1974): 22-23.

21. See Alan Rabwowitz, *Municipal Bond Finance and Administration* (New York: Wiley-Interscience, 1969).

22. U.S. Federal Power Commission, *1970 National Power Survey*, op. cit., p. I-20-9.

23. For an account of the current state of TVA see "Tennessee Valley Authority: The Yardstick With Less Than 36 Inches," *Forbes* 115, no. 7 (April 1, 1975): 24-28.

24. U.S. General Accounting Office, *Examination of Financial Statements of the Tennessee Valley Authority for Fiscal Year 1971* (Washington: U.S. General Accounting Office, 1972), p. 7.

25. U.S. Federal Power Commission, *1970 National Power Survey*, op. cit., p. I-20-9.

26. U.S. Rural Electrification Administration, *Annual Statistical Reports—REA Bulletin 1-1* (Washington: U.S. Government Printing Office, various years).

27. David A. Halm, "Stepping Up the Pace in Financing," *Public Utilities Fortnightly* 96, no. 7 (September 27, 1975): 32-33.

# 5

## PROJECTED FINANCING OF THE ELECTRIC UTILITIES

In recent years concern has been expressed by many over the possible in-ability of various domestic industries to raise funds to support the projected in-crease in capital expenditures during the 1970s and 1980s. Concern has centered on a number of areas including: 1) rapid inflation making depreciation allow-ances insufficient for the replacement of deteriorated and obsolete equipment, 2) a decay in profit margins leading to declines in coverage ratios and bond ratings and an insufficient retained earnings component, 3) a two-tier equities market prohibiting many firms from raising new funds through common stock sales, 4) large federal deficits which will drain away a major portion of the avail-able supply of long-term capital, and 5) a feeling that the capital markets may not be able to facilitate the tremendous flows of money which will be required during the two-decade period. Although these are certainly not the only problem areas for U.S. industry, they represent widespread and important concerns.

In no industry will the stress of raising funds be greater than with the elec-tric utilities. In the *1970 National Power Survey* the Federal Power Commission estimated that the industry's capital requirements during the 1970-90 period would be between $400 billion and $500 billion in 1970 prices.[1] More recent surveys by *Electrical World* placed capital expenditures at somewhat different levels. The 1973 survey estimated capital spending during 1976-90 at approxi-mately $420 billion in 1973 prices,[2] and the 1974 survey showed a decline for the same period to $379 billion in 1974 prices.[3] The Federal Power Commission estimate for the same 15 years, adjusted to 1974 prices, approximates $450 bil-lion and shows the drastic revision in spending plans which occurred during the early 1970s. The three forecasts are illustrated in Figure 5.1 using constant 1974 prices.

A study draft prepared by the National Power Survey Technical Advisory Committee on Finance for the Federal Power Commission, and distributed for

## FIGURE 5.1

### Estimates of Capital Expenditures
### for Electric Utilities, 1976-90
### (constant 1974 dollars)

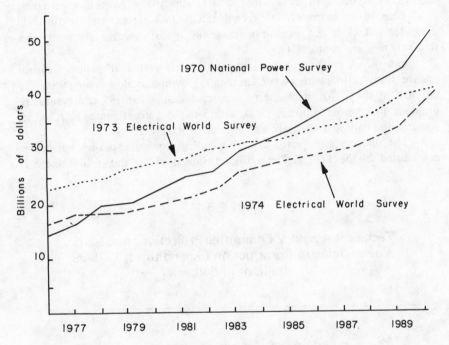

Sources: U.S. Federal Power Commission, *1970 National Power Survey* (Washington: U.S. Government Printing Office, 1971), p. I-20-1; and *Electrical World* 180, no. 6: 53, and 182, no. 6: 57.

discussion in the last quarter of 1974, projected electric power industry construction expenditures for 1975-89 based upon seven possible scenarios.

*Case I*—A moderate growth rate of somewhat lower proportions than in the recent past: 5.5 to 6.5 percent annual growth in peak demand, 5 to 7.5 percent annual increases in construction costs, and relatively high environmental costs.

*Case IA*—The same as Case I except with lower environmental costs.

*Case II*—A continuation of past growth rates, with 6.5 to 7 percent annual growth in peak demand, 5 to 7.5 percent annual increases in construction costs, and relatively low environmental costs.

*Case III*—A low growth rate considerably less than in past years, with 3 to 5 percent annual growth in peak demand, 3 to 7.5 percent annual increases in construction costs, and relatively high environmental costs.

*Case IV*—An "all-electric" economy with growth much higher than in the past, with 8 to 10 percent annual growth in peak demand, 5.5 to 7 percent annual increases in construction costs, and relatively low environmental costs.

*Case V*—An extremely low growth rate, with 1 percent annual growth in peak demand, 3 to 7.5 percent increases in annual construction costs, and relatively high environmental costs.

*Case VI*—A moderate growth rate in the early years that declines throughout the study period, with a 6 percent annual growth in peak demand during the last half of the 1970s, declining to 3 percent during 1981-85 and eventually dropping to 1 percent through 1990, with 3 to 7.5 percent annual increases in construction costs and relatively high environmental costs.

The industry's projected capital spending requirements for each of the cases listed in the Federal Power Commission draft are shown in Table 5.1.

## TABLE 5.1

### Technical Advisory Committee Projections of Electric Power Industry Construction Expenditures, 1975-89 (billions of dollars)

| 5-Year Period | Case I | Case IA | Case II | Case III | Case IV | Case V | Case VI |
|---|---|---|---|---|---|---|---|
| 1975-79 | 139 | 122 | 137 | 101 | 162 | 41 | 116 |
| 1980-84 | 212 | 200 | 238 | 108 | 406 | 27 | 92 |
| 1985-89 | 314 | 298 | 393 | 128 | 686 | 36 | 60 |
| Total | 665 | 620 | 768 | 337 | 1,254 | 104 | 268 |

*Note*: Includes nuclear fuel and allowance for funds used during construction; not reduced by retirements.

*Source*: U.S. Federal Power Commission, Preliminary Partial Draft of the Report of the National Power Survey Technical Advisory Committee on Finance, October 10, 1974.

Depending upon the level of inflation occurring over this span of time, the latest Federal Power Commission study makes it clear that the actual expenditures will be significantly greater than the estimates using constant prices. Using the 1974 *Electrical World* Survey, Table 5.2 illustrates the projected capital requirements under various assumptions of price level changes.

## INVESTOR-OWNED SYSTEMS

While municipal, federal, and cooperative systems are of considerable importance in the generation, and especially the distribution of electric power, most problems will continue to be borne by the investor-owned segment of the industry. From the 1950s through 1970, investor-owned systems increased their share of the industry's total capital expenditures for electric plant from the 70-72 percent range to 81 percent.[4] Should investor-owned systems continue to increase this share of the industry's expenditures at a similar rate, they will be making approximately 92 percent of capital expenditures for electric plant by 1990. Assuming that this trend occurs, the capital requirements at various levels of inflation over the 15-year span are displayed in Table 5.3. Even at inflation rates considered reasonably moderate by present-day standards, the effect of potential price level changes on expenditures is huge. Required spending of $338 billion is constant 1974 dollars would be magnified to $512 billion under 4 percent inflation, $633 billion with 6 percent inflation, and $793 billion if 8 percent inflation occurs—increases of 51, 87 and 132 percent, respectively. Inflation rates of the magnitude experienced in 1973 and 1974 would produce correspondingly larger capital spending requirements.

## TABLE 5.2

### Capital Requirements in the Electric Power Industry at Various Levels of Inflation, 1976-90

| Rate of Inflation (percent) | Capital Requirement (billions of dollars) |
| --- | --- |
| 1974 Prices | 379 |
| 4 | 572 |
| 5 | 636 |
| 6 | 705 |
| 7 | 784 |
| 8 | 871 |

*Source*: Calculated from "25th Annual Electrical Industry Forecast," *Electrical World* 182, no. 6 (September 15, 1974): 57.

## TABLE 5.3

Capital Requirements for Investor-Owned Electric Utilities at Various Levels of Inflation, 1976-90
(millions of dollars)

| Year | 1974 Dollars | Rate of Inflation (percent) | | | | |
|---|---|---|---|---|---|---|
| | | 4 | 5 | 6 | 7 | 8 |
| 1976 | 13,849 | 14,985 | 15,262 | 15,566 | 15,857 | 16,148 |
| 1977 | 14,462 | 16,270 | 16,747 | 17,224 | 17,716 | 18,220 |
| 1978 | 14,903 | 17,437 | 18,793 | 18,808 | 19,538 | 20,268 |
| 1979 | 15,375 | 18,711 | 19,618 | 20,572 | 21,571 | 22,586 |
| 1980 | 16,855 | 21,322 | 22,626 | 23,917 | 25,299 | 26,749 |
| 1981 | 19,046 | 25,065 | 26,798 | 28,645 | 30,588 | 32,645 |
| 1982 | 21,026 | 28,785 | 31,055 | 33,515 | 36,123 | 38,919 |
| 1983 | 22,368 | 31,830 | 34,693 | 37,780 | 41,112 | 44,714 |
| 1984 | 23,371 | 34,589 | 38,071 | 41,857 | 45,971 | 50,458 |
| 1985 | 23,605 | 36,397 | 40,442 | 44,888 | 49,783 | 55,152 |
| 1986 | 25,929 | 41,512 | 46,568 | 52,169 | 58,392 | 65,289 |
| 1987 | 28,235 | 47,124 | 52,658 | 60,310 | 68,187 | 76,799 |
| 1988 | 30,570 | 52,672 | 60,529 | 69,119 | 78,840 | 89,784 |
| 1989 | 32,934 | 59,314 | 68,470 | 78,943 | 90,865 | 104,467 |
| 1990 | 35,326 | 66,166 | 77,117 | 89,728 | 104,282 | 121,027 |
| Total | 337,899 | 512,179 | 569,447 | 633,041 | 704,124 | 783,225 |

*Source:* Capital spending estimates in constant prices from "25th Annual Electrical Industry Forecast," *Electrical World* 182, no. 6 (September 15, 1974): 57.

to $155 billion, while providing only 19.8 percent of total funding. Conversely, a lower rate of price level changes would result in reduced depreciation charges, but at the same time increase the percentage contribution of this source. Projected annual funding requirements provided by depreciation at various rates of inflation are contained in Appendix A.

## TABLE 5.4

### Projected Annual Depreciation and Capital Requirements for Investor-Owned Electric Utilities at 6 Percent Inflation, 1976-90 (millions of dollars)

| Year | Capital Requirements | Depreciation | Percent of Funds Provided by Depreciation |
|------|---------------------|--------------|-------------------------------------------|
| 1976 | 15,566 | 4,335 | 27.8 |
| 1977 | 17,224 | 4,683 | 27.2 |
| 1978 | 18,808 | 5,065 | 26.9 |
| 1979 | 20,572 | 5,483 | 26.6 |
| 1980 | 23,917 | 5,981 | 25.0 |
| 1981 | 28,645 | 6,593 | 23.0 |
| 1982 | 33,515 | 7,320 | 21.8 |
| 1983 | 37,780 | 8,142 | 21.5 |
| 1984 | 41,857 | 9,053 | 21.6 |
| 1985 | 44,888 | 10,020 | 22.3 |
| 1986 | 52,169 | 11,158 | 21.4 |
| 1987 | 60,310 | 12,485 | 20.7 |
| 1988 | 69,119 | 14,014 | 20.3 |
| 1989 | 78,943 | 15,768 | 19.9 |
| 1990 | 89,728 | 17,764 | 19.8 |
| Total | 633,041 | 137,864 | 21.8 |

*Sources:* Capital requirements calculated from projections by *Electrical World*; remaining data compiled by author.

The contribution of depreciation would be altered depending upon variations in tax laws, depreciation practices, and asset mix during the period of study. For example, hydroelectric facilities typically have a longer lifespan than steam-electric plants, and are thus depreciated at a significantly lower rate.[7] Should the former become less important as additions to generating capacity come on-line, the 2.7 percent aggregate depreciation rate would tend to increase.

*Retained Earnings*

Since retained earnings represent the net profits which are reinvested in the industry rather than paid out as cash dividends, calculation of this variable requires an estimation of profits after taxes and dividends during the 1976-90 period. The dividends are then subtracted from net profits to obtain this second internal source of funds.

To estimate net income, historical data for investor-owned electric utilities were used. Figures for profits after taxes were found for each year from 1950 to 1972 using composite income accounts of the industry.[8] The return on aggregate net utility assets was then computed by dividing net income by net assets.[9] Over the 23-year period, the after-tax return averaged 4.30 percent of net assets with a standard deviation of .22 percent. Results of the calculations of return on net assets are displayed in Table 5.5.

## TABLE 5.5

### Return on Net Assets for Investor-Owned Electric Utilities, 1950-72

| Range of Return on Net Assets (percent) | Percent of Times in Range |
| --- | --- |
| 4.2 to 4.4 | 26 |
| 4.1 to 4.5 | 57 |
| 4.0 to 4.6 | 78 |

*Source*: U.S. Federal Power Commission, *Statistics of Privately Owned Electric Utilities, 1972* (Washington, U.S. Government Printing Office, 1974).

Hence, 57 percent of the time the return on net assets for investor-owned electric utilities has been between 4.1 percent and 4.5 percent, and 78 percent of the time the return has been between 4.0 percent and 4.6 percent over the 23-year span.

To project net profits on an annual basis during the 1976-90 period, it is necessary to first estimate net assets during each year. This was done in the previous section in calculating yearly depreciation allowances and is therefore available for use in projecting the remaining internal funding source. Projected net profits at an assumed 6 percent rate of inflation for 1976 through 1990 are found in Table 5.6.

To derive retained earnings it is necessary to subtract estimated dividend payments from the net income projections of Table 5.6. From 1950 through 1972, preferred dividends averaged slightly over 10 percent of after-tax income, while cash dividends on common stock averaged approximately 71 percent of

# TABLE 5.6

Projected Net Profits with 6 Percent Inflation for Investor-Owned Electric Utilities, 1976-90
(millions of dollars)

| Year | Return on Net Assets (percent) | | | | | | |
| | 4.0 | 4.1 | 4.2 | 4.3 | 4.4 | 4.5 | 4.6 |
|---|---|---|---|---|---|---|---|
| 1976 | 6,249 | 6,406 | 6,562 | 6,718 | 6,874 | 7,031 | 7,187 |
| 1977 | 6,751 | 6,902 | 7,088 | 7,257 | 7,426 | 7,595 | 7,764 |
| 1978 | 7,301 | 7,483 | 7,666 | 7,848 | 8,031 | 8,213 | 8,396 |
| 1979 | 7,904 | 8,102 | 8,300 | 8,497 | 8,695 | 8,892 | 9,090 |
| 1980 | 8,622 | 8,837 | 9,053 | 9,268 | 9,484 | 9,700 | 9,915 |
| 1981 | 9,504 | 9,741 | 9,979 | 10,217 | 10,454 | 10,692 | 10,929 |
| 1982 | 10,552 | 10,815 | 11,079 | 11,343 | 11,607 | 11,871 | 12,134 |
| 1983 | 11,737 | 12,031 | 12,324 | 12,617 | 12,911 | 13,204 | 13,498 |
| 1984 | 13,049 | 13,376 | 13,702 | 14,028 | 14,354 | 14,680 | 15,007 |
| 1985 | 14,444 | 14,805 | 15,166 | 15,527 | 15,888 | 16,250 | 16,611 |
| 1986 | 16,084 | 16,487 | 16,889 | 17,291 | 17,693 | 18,095 | 18,497 |
| 1987 | 17,997 | 18,447 | 18,897 | 19,347 | 19,797 | 20,247 | 20,697 |
| 1988 | 20,202 | 20,707 | 21,212 | 21,717 | 22,222 | 22,727 | 23,232 |
| 1989 | 22,729 | 23,297 | 23,865 | 24,433 | 25,002 | 25,570 | 26,138 |
| 1990 | 25,607 | 26,247 | 26,888 | 27,528 | 28,168 | 28,808 | 29,448 |
| Total | 198,732 | 203,701 | 208,670 | 213,636 | 218,606 | 223,575 | 228,543 |

*Source:* Compiled by author.

earnings available for common stock.[10] The combination of preferred and common stock cash dividends averaged nearly 73.5 percent of net income over the 22-year period, and slightly over 75.5 percent since 1937. Should investor-owned utilities keep preferred stock at approximately the same relative importance in their capital structures, the preferred payout will increase throughout future years due to the higher rate of return new issues must yield to investors. The trend to a higher payout was sharply evident in 1971 and 1972, when preferred stock dividends represented 12.8 percent and 14.3 percent of net income, respectively. The matrix for retained earnings shown in Table 5.7 assumes that preferred plus common stock cash dividends will be at a rate of 75.5 percent of net income from 1976 through 1990. In addition, a 6 percent rate of inflation is assumed as it was in calculating the net income of Table 5.6.

While a 4.3 percent rate of return has been the average and will be used in estimating external funding requirements through 1990, it is somewhat surprising to note the retained earnings component is not significantly affected by what rate of return the industry earns within the range shown. For example, a return of 4.6 percent, which is abnormally high by historical standards, rather than 4.3 percent, would provide only $3,657 million in additional funds over the 15-year period. This is relatively insignificant when compared with the $633 billion in capital expenditures required during the same years. On the other hand, should the return on net assets fall from 4.3 percent to 4.0 percent, aggregate retained earnings would fall only from $52.3 billion to $48.7 billion throughout the 15 years. In reality, however, an increasing rate of return on assets would probably result in a lower dividend payout ratio as earnings increased faster than dividend payments. Consequently, the retained earnings figures, but not the net income figures, of Table 5.7 are somewhat understated at high rates of return and overstated at low rates of return.

A much more significant factor in determining the dollar amount of funds generated through retained earnings will be the rate of inflation which prevails from 1976 until 1990. For example, Table 5.8 shows that if prices increase at a rate of 8 percent, rather than 6 percent, aggregate funds reinvested in the industry from profits will jump from $52.3 billion to $57.5 billion, with a constant 4.3 percent return on net assets. Unfortunately, inflation would cause capital requirements over the 15-year span to increase by $150 billion to a level of slightly over $783 billion. Should the rate of inflation decline to 4 percent, the contribution from retained earnings would drop from $52.3 billion to $47.2 billion, at a return of 4.3 percent on net assets. However, required capital expenditures would decline by 24 times the reduction in retained earnings, from $633 billion to $512 billion. A more detailed breakdown of net profit and retained earnings projections on an annual basis can be found in Appendix B.

## TABLE 5.7

Projected Retained Earnings with 6 Percent Inflation for Investor-Owned Electric Utilities, 1976-90
(millions of dollars)

| Year | Return on Net Assets (percent) | | | | | | |
|---|---|---|---|---|---|---|---|
| | 4.0 | 4.1 | 4.2 | 4.3 | 4.4 | 4.5 | 4.6 |
| 1976 | 1,531 | 1,570 | 1,608 | 1,646 | 1,684 | 1,723 | 1,761 |
| 1977 | 1,654 | 1,695 | 1,737 | 1,778 | 1,819 | 1,861 | 1,903 |
| 1978 | 1,789 | 1,833 | 1,878 | 1,923 | 1,968 | 2,012 | 2,057 |
| 1979 | 1,937 | 1,985 | 2,034 | 2,082 | 2,130 | 2,179 | 2,227 |
| 1980 | 2,112 | 2,165 | 2,218 | 2,271 | 2,324 | 2,376 | 2,429 |
| 1981 | 2,329 | 2,387 | 2,445 | 2,503 | 2,561 | 2,620 | 2,678 |
| 1982 | 2,585 | 2,650 | 2,714 | 2,779 | 2,844 | 2,908 | 2,973 |
| 1983 | 2,876 | 2,948 | 3,019 | 3,091 | 3,163 | 3,235 | 3,307 |
| 1984 | 3,197 | 3,277 | 3,357 | 3,437 | 3,517 | 3,597 | 3,677 |
| 1985 | 3,539 | 3,627 | 3,716 | 3,804 | 3,893 | 3,981 | 4,070 |
| 1986 | 3,941 | 4,039 | 4,138 | 4,236 | 4,335 | 4,433 | 4,532 |
| 1987 | 4,409 | 4,520 | 4,630 | 4,740 | 4,850 | 4,961 | 5,071 |
| 1988 | 4,950 | 5,073 | 5,197 | 5,321 | 5,444 | 5,568 | 5,698 |
| 1989 | 5,569 | 5,708 | 5,847 | 5,986 | 6,126 | 6,265 | 6,406 |
| 1990 | 6,274 | 6,431 | 6,588 | 6,744 | 6,901 | 7,058 | 7,215 |
| Total | 48,692 | 49,908 | 51,126 | 52,341 | 53,559 | 54,777 | 55,998 |

*Source:* Compiled by author.

## TABLE 5.8

### Investor-Owned Electric Utility Aggregate Net Profits and Retained Earnings at Various Returns on Investment and Various Rates of Inflation, 1976-90
(millions of dollars)

| Return on Net Investment (percent) | Rate of Inflation (percent) | | | | |
|---|---|---|---|---|---|
| | 4 | 5 | 6 | 7 | 8 |
| Net Profits | | | | | |
| 4.0 | 179,205 | 188,977 | 198,732 | 208,499 | 218,264 |
| 4.1 | 183,686 | 193,698 | 203,701 | 213,710 | 223,718 |
| 2.4 | 188,167 | 198,425 | 208,670 | 218,923 | 229,174 |
| 4.3 | 192,645 | 203,149 | 213,636 | 224,136 | 234,633 |
| 4.4 | 197,124 | 207,873 | 218,926 | 229,349 | 240,089 |
| 4.5 | 201,605 | 212,599 | 223,575 | 234,559 | 245,543 |
| 4.6 | 206,086 | 217,324 | 228,543 | 239,772 | 251,001 |
| Retained Earnings | | | | | |
| 4.0 | 43,905 | 46,300 | 48,692 | 51,082 | 53,475 |
| 4.1 | 45,000 | 47,454 | 49,908 | 52,359 | 54,811 |
| 4.2 | 46,141 | 48,607 | 51,126 | 53,636 | 56,148 |
| 4.3 | 47,198 | 49,770 | 52,341 | 54,913 | 57,485 |
| 4.4 | 48,294 | 50,931 | 53,559 | 56,191 | 58,822 |
| 4.5 | 49,394 | 52,087 | 54,777 | 57,467 | 60,158 |
| 4.6 | 50,491 | 53,245 | 55,998 | 58,744 | 61,495 |

*Source*: Compiled by author.

## External Sources of Funds

If the aforementioned projections are accurate and investor-owned systems continue to earn 4.3 percent on net assets and pay slightly over 75 percent of net earnings in cash dividends, the internally generated sources of depreciation and retained earnings should provide slightly over $190 billion during 1976-90. This would mean that this group of utilities would be required to raise nearly $443 billion in external funds during the same period. The 69.9 percent of total financing requirements to flow from external sources, which is necessitated by this projection, is in contrast to 60.2 percent during the 25 years from 1948-72. It is, however, in line with financing methods used during 1970, 1971, and 1972. An annual breakdown of sources of funds from 1976 through 1990 is found in Table 5.9.

# TABLE 5.9

## Projected Sources of Funds for Investor-Owned Electric Utilities, 1976-90
### (millions of dollars)

| Year | Capital Requirements[a] | Depreciation | Retained Earnings[b] | External Sources | Percent External |
|------|------------------------|--------------|----------------------|------------------|------------------|
| 1976 | 15,556 | 4,335 | 1,646 | 9,585 | 61.6 |
| 1977 | 17,224 | 4,683 | 1,778 | 10,763 | 62.5 |
| 1978 | 18,808 | 5,065 | 1,923 | 11,820 | 62.8 |
| 1979 | 20,572 | 5,483 | 2,082 | 13,007 | 63.2 |
| 1980 | 23,917 | 5,981 | 2,271 | 15,665 | 65.5 |
| 1981 | 28,645 | 6,593 | 2,503 | 19,549 | 68.2 |
| 1982 | 33,515 | 7,320 | 2,779 | 23,416 | 69.9 |
| 1983 | 37,780 | 8,142 | 3,091 | 26,547 | 70.3 |
| 1984 | 41,857 | 9,053 | 3,437 | 29,367 | 70.2 |
| 1985 | 44,888 | 10,020 | 3,804 | 31,064 | 69.2 |
| 1986 | 52,169 | 11,158 | 4,236 | 36,775 | 70.5 |
| 1987 | 60,310 | 12,485 | 4,740 | 43,085 | 71.4 |
| 1988 | 69,119 | 14,014 | 5,321 | 49,784 | 72.0 |
| 1989 | 78,943 | 15,768 | 5,986 | 57,189 | 72.4 |
| 1990 | 89,728 | 17,764 | 6,774 | 65,220 | 72.7 |
| Total | 633,401 | 137,864 | 52,341 | 442,836 | 69.9 |

[a]Projected capital expenditures assume an annual 6 percent inflation rate.
[b]Based upon the assumptions that net earnings average 4.3 percent of net assets and that the industry pays 75.5 percent of earnings in common and preferred cash dividends.

*Sources:* Capital requirements calculated from projections by *Electrical World*; remaining data compiled by author.

87

Perhaps the most disconcerting part of the forecast is that the portion of funds to be raised outside the industry increases in each year. While 1976 shows that 38.4 percent of total funds will be raised through internal sources, by 1990 depreciation and retained earnings will contribute only 27.3 percent of capital requirements. This is a smaller portion than the industry has generated in any year since 1948, when only 26.4 percent of total funds were obtained internally.[11]

As mentioned earlier, a rate of return slightly higher than the average 4.3 percent used in this study does not have a significant impact upon the amount of total funds which must be raised externally, although it may make the acquisition of these funds considerably easier. Table 5.10 illustrates that even with an abnormally high return of 4.6 percent, over 69 percent of total capital requirements will have to be financed through common stock, preferred stock, and debt sales. The small change in the amount of internal funding due to higher rates of return occurs because depreciation, the largest internal source, is unaffected by the rate of return, and because a large portion of the increase in net profits is projected to be paid out in cash dividends. In order to keep external requirements at 60 percent of total funding, the industry would have to generate

## TABLE 5.10

### External Financing Requirements and Rates of Return with 6 Percent Inflation, 1976-90

| Rate of Return (percent) | External Funds Required (millions of dollars) | Percent External |
|---|---|---|
| 4.0 | 446,485 | 70.5 |
| 4.1 | 445,269 | 70.3 |
| 4.2 | 444,051 | 70.1 |
| 4.3 | 442,836 | 70.0 |
| 4.4 | 441,618 | 69.8 |
| 4.5 | 400,400 | 69.6 |
| 4.6 | 439,179 | 69.4 |

Source: Compiled by author.

slightly over $115 billion in retained earnings. If a 75.5 percent payout ratio was to continue, this would require that the investor-owned utilities earn profits of approximately $470 billion or a 9.46 percent return on net assets.

The percentage of aggregate industry capital requirements supplied by the publicly owned electric utilities also affects the internal-external split, since it determines the amount of funds which investor-owned systems must raise in a given year. For example, if public and cooperative systems continue to control approximately 20 percent of industry investments, rather than decline in importance as has been assumed, the required fund raising of private utilities over the 15 years would be reduced to $577 billion from $633 billion as shown in Table 5.4. However, the reduction in capital expenditures would result in fewer assets each year, so that depreciation and net profits would also be less than previously estimated. Under this scenario internal sources provide nearly $180 billion, or 31.1 percent of total capital requirements, compared to the $190 billion or 30.1 percent in Table 5.9. Thus, while capital investment needs would fall by $56 billion, $10 billion of the decline is represented by internal funds which would not accrue to the private sector because of the reduced outlays. External funding would become increasingly important throughout the period and by 1990, investor-owned systems would find it necessary to raise slightly over 72 percent of total financing requirements through new stock and bond issues.

Over the past 35 years, debt in the capital structure of investor-owned electric utilities has ranged from a low of 46.1 percent in 1946 to a high of 54.8 percent in 1970. Figures for selected years are illustrated in Table 5.11. Although there has been a clear long-term trend toward incorporating additional debt into capital structures, evidence has begun to appear that a peak may have been reached, or at least approached, in 1970. Beginning in the early 1970s,

## TABLE 5.11

### Debt as a Percentage of Total Capitalization for Investor-Owned Electric Utilities, 1940-72

| Year | Percent Debt |
|------|--------------|
| 1940 | 47.3 |
| 1945 | 46.5 |
| 1950 | 48.9 |
| 1955 | 50.7 |
| 1960 | 52.8 |
| 1965 | 51.5 |
| 1970 | 54.8 |
| 1971 | 54.2 |
| 1972 | 53.1 |

*Source*: Federal Power Commission, *Statistics of Privately Owned Electric Utilities in the United States* (Washington: U.S. Government Printing Office, various years).

utilities began issuing increasing amounts of preferred and common stock so that the percentage of debt actually declined in 1971 and 1972.

Interest coverage ratios declined dramatically throughout the 1960s and early 1970s and, even if the proportion of debt is not increased further, a continuing deterioration may be expected to occur as new higher interest bearing securities are issued to raise new funds and to replace maturing debt. With the assumptions that debt will reach a maximum of 55 percent of capitalization, and that retained earnings will total $52 billion from 1976 through 1990 (see Table 5.8), the $443 billion in required external funds will be raised by issuing approximately $170 billion in common and preferred stock and $273 billion in long-term debt. Proportionately, this new funding of approximately 38 percent equity and 62 percent debt is more heavily weighted toward the latter than was the case in the early 1970s. However, the $170 billion in common and preferred stock financing throughout the 15-year period is over six times as much equity as was issued by investor-owned systems in the 25 years from 1948 to 1972.

A somewhat more reasonable assumption, perhaps, is a capitalization composed of 50 percent debt and 50 percent equity. This result could be obtained by issuing $247 billion in debt and $196 billion in preferred and common stock. These and other capitalization ratios are contained in Table 5.12.

## TABLE 5.12

Investor-Owned Electric Utility Equity and Debt Issues to Achieve Target Capitalization Ratios, 1976-90

| Percent Debt in Capital Structure | Equity Issues (billions of dollars) | Debt Issues (billions of dollars) |
|---|---|---|
| 45 | 220 | 223 |
| 46 | 215 | 228 |
| 47 | 210 | 233 |
| 48 | 205 | 238 |
| 49 | 200 | 243 |
| 50 | 196 | 247 |
| 51 | 191 | 252 |
| 52 | 186 | 257 |
| 53 | 181 | 262 |
| 54 | 176 | 267 |
| 55 | 170 | 273 |

Source: Compiled by author.

Whatever capitalization ratio is achieved, the amounts of debt and equity issued by investor-owned electric utilities through 1990 will be huge. The $443 billion in external funds required in the 1976-90 period compares with total gross utility plant of $127 billion at the end of 1972. The only alternative available to reduce the amounts of outside equity and debt which will be required are a greater contribution from internal funding, reduced capital spending requirements, or increasing reliance on public and cooperative systems.

## PUBLICLY AND COOPERATIVELY OWNED SYSTEMS

Incorporating the original assumptions of $706 billion in industry expenditures (with 6 percent inflation) and an increasing penetration of the investor-owned segment results in approximately $73 billion in capital spending by public and cooperative systems.

It seems difficult to imagine any sizable problem in financing the federal systems since contributions, with the exception of TVA bonds, are made by the U.S. Treasury. Although the potential spending needs of these utilities must compete with alternative federal programs, these appropriations can be expected to continue nearly unabated as expansion requirements rise over the years. A more difficult situation may develop in the market for tax-exempt bonds issued by nonfederal public systems. There has been some concern voiced that the market for these securities will become saturated as municipal governments issue increasing amounts of debt to finance spending programs. This may be even more the case since industrial revenue bonds used to finance pollution-abatement facilities now qualify for tax-exempt status. At the present time, however, tax-exempt debt offerings to finance capital expenditures for public utilities comprise only a small portion of the total volume of tax-exempt offerings. While the cost of this debt relative to taxable securities has risen somewhat in recent years, public systems should find sufficient funds for expansion. In fact, as inflation forces people into higher tax brackets it is quite possible that the spread in interest rates between nontaxable and taxable securities might actually widen.[12]

Perhaps the greatest difficulty in raising capital for expansion among non-investor-owned utilities will be borne by the cooperatives. Due to the need to obtain supplemental financing from nongovernmental sources as a condition for obtaining a Rural Electrification Administration loan, this segment of the industry could well experience rapidly escalating costs and deteriorating financial ratios. To aid cooperatives in finding supplemental loans the National Rural Utilities Cooperative Finance Corporation has been established. This organization should become a significant factor in financing this segment of the industry. Should the cooperatives experience problems in raising funds for capital spending, they might well begin buying more power for resale to consumers, thereby putting even more pressure on other segments of the industry.

## NOTES

1. U.S. Federal Power Commission, *1970 National Power Survey* (Washington: U.S. Government Printing Office, 1971), p. I-20-1.

2. Reprinted from September 15, 1973 issue of *Electrical World* Copyright 1973, McGraw-Hill, Inc. All rights reserved.

3. Reprinted from September 15, 1974 issue of *Electrical World* Copyright 1974, McGraw-Hill, Inc. All rights reserved.

4. U.S. Federal Power Commission, op. cit., p. I-20-1.

5. U.S. Federal Power Commission, *Statistics of Privately Owned Electric Utilities in the United States* (Washington: U.S. Government Printing Office, various years).

6. Leonard M. Olmsted, "Utilities Slash Spending Plans," *Electrical World* 182, no. 6 (September 15, 1974): 57.

7. U.S. Federal Power Commission, *1970 National Power Survey*, op. cit., p. I-20-7.

8. ———, *Statistics of Privately Owned Electric Utilities in the United States, 1972* (Washington: U.S. Government Printing Office, 1974), p. XXIX.

9. Ibid., p. XXII.

10. Ibid., p. XXIX.

11 U.S. Federal Power Commission, *1970 National Power Survey*, op. cit., p. I-20-6.

12. See Sanford Rose, "The Trouble With Municipal Bonds Is Not Just New York," *Fortune* 92, no. 6 (December 1975): 104-07, 176-82.

# 6

## SUMMARY, CONCLUSIONS, AND RECOMMENDATIONS

While primary energy consumption in the United States has expanded rapidly, it has been consistently outpaced by growth in the usage of electric power. The latter has been growing at a rate of approximately 7 percent annually, or doubling in use every decade. Electricity is a convenient, clean (at the point of consumption) and, in many cases, necessary form of energy.

The electric utility industry is structured into four distinct ownership segments, of which the investor-owned systems are dominant in nearly every category except the number of firms. These private systems service over 78 percent of all electric customers and own nearly 80 percent of the industry's total generating capacity. Nearly all of the largest investor-owned companies are integrated and provide facilities for generation, transmission, and distribution.

The remaining three segments of the industry—public nonfederal, federal, and cooperative—service customers throughout the United States. Public nonfederal systems are involved primarily in reselling power, although a number of the large metropolitan utilities also generate most or all of their needs. Federal systems are second only to the investor-owned segment in generating electricity which, for the most part, is integrated into other electric systems and sold at wholesale rates. Cooperative utilities are involved primarily in reselling electric power purchased from private and federal installations. There has been a trend in recent years toward the building of generation and transmission facilities by this segment of the industry.

In order to improve reliability and minimize costs, nearly all major electric systems are interconnected in an effort to coordinate activities. Various types of coordination involve staggered plant construction, joint ownership of facilities, and the sharing of reserve capacity. In contrast to these formal power pools, less involved cooperative agreements may provide for no more than the free exchange of information. As the cost of providing power has risen, coordination has received increasing attention by nearly all electric utility systems.

Electric power systems are regulated at both the federal level and through state and local regulatory commissions. The former includes the involvement of a number of agencies including the Federal Power Commission, the Securities and Exchange Commission, the Atomic Energy Commission, and the Environmental Protection Agency. Jurisdiction by these groups ranges from safety requirements to regulation of interstate wholesale rates. State and local regulatory bodies are generally concerned with the return to nonfederal systems. The return is dependent upon the valuation of assets included in the rate base, the deductions which are allowed from operating revenues, and the percentage rate of return which is permitted. The Supreme Court ruling in the *Hope Natural Gas* case gave commissions relatively wide discretion in rate-making. Consequently, the return allowed among electric utilities has varied greatly.

Nearly 80 percent of all electric power is generated by the burning of fossil fuels. Coal remains the most important primary energy source in powering generation equipment, although both oil and gas have increased in relative usage over the past 25 years. Due to the shortage of natural gas and numerous problems with oil, coal is expected to provide the largest share of fossil fuel power in future years.

Nuclear power is just beginning to supply a significant portion of base-load requirements, while hydro facilities, although possessing many desirable attributes, have continued declining in relative importance since 1935. This trend is expected by most observers to continue throughout the remainder of this century. The Federal Power Commission Task Force on Utility Fuels Requirements projects that by the year 2000 the energy source generation mix will be comprised of 5 percent hydro power, 62 percent nuclear fuels, and 33 percent fossil fuels. Fossil fuel inputs consist of 61 percent coal, 4 percent gas, and 15 percent oil.[1]

In addition to the conventional and nuclear steam plants and hydro facilities which currently provide base-load requirements, alternative production methods such as diesels and geothermal energy contribute small amounts of power. Promising research is underway on both solar and fusion power as possible large-scale energy sources for future years.

All methods of generating electric power produce residuals which have undesirable effects upon the environment. These include impacts upon air quality, water quality, and land use.[2] It is unfortunate that the types of plants offering the cleanest method of generating electricity—hydroelectric and gas-fired steam plants—are also the ones which will offer a declining contribution to total supply. Coal-fired generating facilities, which will be increasingly relied upon, present especially severe environmental problems.

## COST TRENDS

Until the late 1960s, the average price of electricity to consumers had been declining despite rising prices in other sectors of the economy. This decline was due to an actual fall in the price of electricity through the early 1960s, and also to the price structure traditionally employed by the industry. The declining block-rate structure rewards large users with lower per-kilowatt costs.

Beginning in the late 1960s, technological improvements and scale economies could no longer overcome rapidly increasing capital costs and fuel expenses, causing the price of electric power to consumers to rise. While increased fuel costs were passed through quickly by the fuel adjustment clauses, higher capital costs were, to a large extent, absorbed by the utilities due to regulatory lag. Had these latter increases been passed on in the manner of fuel expenses, the rise in the cost of electricity would have been even more dramatic.

Inflation has had a severe impact upon capital costs of electric utilities. Projections for nuclear plants to come on-line in the early 1980s estimate costs at over $700 per kilowatt. Cost estimates for coal-fired plants for commercial operation in the same period are over $600 per kilowatt. This compares with a 1967 Atomic Energy Commission projection for 1972 operation of $134 and $100 per kilowatt, respectively.[3] It should be noted that the 1967 estimate was in constant prices, while the more recent projection included a factor for cost escalation.

The electric utility industry is tremendously capital intensive. Companies engaged in the production of electric power must spend nearly $4.50 for assets to produce a dollar of revenue, compared with all manufacturing industries which spend only $.60 per dollar of revenue. It is this large amount of fixed expenses which has guided financial policies of the industry.

Economies of scale are still important in plant and unit size although the cost variation is dependent upon the type of plant being considered. Nuclear plants offer greater scale economies than fossil-fuel plants, although the former are still considerably more expensive at any given plant size.

The cost of protecting the environment has not been cheap for electric power companies. In addition to the extra capital expenditures required to install equipment such as cooling towers, electrostatic precipitators, separators, scrubbers, and underground distribution lines, substantial operating costs and reliability problems have been encountered. Spending on safety-related items has also contributed to rising costs, especially with respect to nuclear plants. It is estimated that cost increases caused by environmental and safety changes between 1971 and 1973 added nearly $34 to the cost of a 1,000-megawatt light-water reactor plant.[4]

Beginning in the early 1970s, fuel cost increases became an area of major concern for the industry. The problem was particularly acute for systems which relied primarily on oil-burning plants, as this fuel increased in cost by over 500 percent between 1969 and 1974. Cost increases in coal and gas were approximately 170 percent and 100 percent, respectively, during the same period. Due to these large increases, fuel costs absorbed nearly 35 percent of electric utility revenues in 1974—a jump from only 20 percent four years earlier.

## HISTORICAL FINANCING

As capital spending increased from $3 billion in 1948 to over $20 billion in 1974, electric utilities found it increasingly necessary to frequent the money markets. Vast amounts of new equity and debt issues were needed to supplement inadequate retained earnings and depreciation allowances.

Investor-owned systems account for approximately 80 percent of the industry's total capital expenditures. These companies raise money in a manner similar to any other private corporation in that funds are generated internally from operations and externally through borrowing and selling ownership. As spending requirements began rising rapidly in the late 1960s and early 1970s, an increasing proportion of capital was raised externally. While long-term borrowing and equity sales had supported 40 percent of capital needs in 1962, they were needed for 70 percent of capital requirements by the early 1970s. The greatest relative decline in internal funding occurred through depreciation allowances, which supplied over 41 percent of total requirements in 1962, but only half that in 1972. Such a trend is to be expected in any period when spending is going through a period of expansion since the amount of depreciation is determined primarily by the depreciable asset base that can change only gradually as new assets are added. During a time of declining capital spending, depreciation would supply an increasing proportion of funds. While depreciation is a relatively stable source of funds, the contribution of retained earnings is somewhat more erratic. Since utilities take pride in liberal and consistent cash dividends, a relatively small proportionate change in earnings results in a relatively large change in retained earnings. The trend of this source has been toward providing a smaller relative contribution of total financing requirements. In 1972 it amounted to only slightly over 8 percent of capital expenditures.

Electric utilities have typically been forced to raise a larger proportion of funds through equity and debt issues than other nonfinancial corporations. This has been especially true in recent years, when these sources yielded up to 70 percent of total funds. Debt has consistently occupied the most important position in the capital structures of the utilities. From under 50 percent of total capitalization in the early 1950s, long-term debt gradually increased to nearly 55 percent in 1970. Net issues were placed at a rate of almost $5 billion annually from 1970 through 1972, an increase from between $1 billion and $2 billion per year in the 1950s and early 1960s.[5] This increase in debt, combined with much higher interest rates, resulted in declining coverage ratios and lower bond ratings.

As long-term debt increased in the utilities' capital structures, preferred stock declined. After representing over 13 percent of capitalization in the early 1950s, preferred stock dropped to less than 10 percent from 1964 through 1970. Beginning in the early 1970s, however, the use of preferred stock was revived, and in 1972 net issues reached well over $2 billion annually. While the portion of the equity base represented by preferred stock has been eroding over the last 25 years, common equity has remained relatively steady. This component includes both earnings retained after dividends and net issues of the new common stock. If retained earnings do not grow to keep pace with an expanding capital base, new common stock can be sold to compensate for the short-fall, and keep common equity at a relatively constant proportion of capitalization. Common stock issues averaged nearly $2.3 billion annually from 1970 through 1972, up from an average of slightly over $500 million during the 1960s.

Municipal utilities raise funds externally through long-term debt and municipal contributions, and internally from depreciation and surplus. Internal sources have generally provided the majority of total spending requirements, but debt issues have become increasingly important and have been used to finance a large amount of new capital assets. Long-term debt issued in 1972 amounted to nearly $850 million as compared to approximately $245 million annually during the mid-1960s.

All federal agencies that are engaged in the generation or distribution of electrical power, except the Tennessee Valley Authority, rely upon congressional appropriations for funding requirements. The Tennessee Valley Authority has received proprietary capital from the federal government and has been allowed to sell its own debt issues in the capital markets.

Cooperatives raise long-term capital from member contributions, loans (primarily from the Rural Electrification Administration), margins, and depreciation allowances. Of these four sources, Rural Electrification Administration loans have supplied the bulk of capital requirements, although in recent years cooperatives have been required to seek supplemental financing from nongovernmental sources.

## FUTURE FINANCING

As in the case with nearly any long-term projections, estimates of the capital needs of the electric power industry are in a constant state of flux. Typically, the tendency has been to underestimate both growth and spending requirements of the industry. However, recent industry financial problems, combined with a drop in demand from consumers, have rendered capital requirement forecasts made in the early 1970s somewhat high. For example, the 1973 forecast by *Electrical World* estimated capital spending by the industry in 1980 and 1985 at $25.1 billion and $29.6 billion, respectively. A year later the estimate was revised to $19.5 billion and $26.4 billion.[6] The revision is even larger than it appears, since the former projections are in 1973 prices and the later estimates in 1974 prices.

The 1974 forecast by *Electrical World* estimates 1976-90 aggregate capital requirements of the electric power industry at approximately $380 billion. When adjusted for inflation, the projected needs are considerably greater. For example, 8 percent inflation over the 15-year period would more than double the necessary funds.

Of the total capital required by the industry, investor-owned systems will need to raise the vast majority of funds. In Chapter 5 it was estimated that this segment of the industry will require nearly $340 billion (in 1974 dollars) if it continues to increase its penetration of the industry. With a 6 percent rate of inflation this would jump to $633 billion. Of this $633 billion capital requirement by the investor-owned sector, depreciation will provide $138 billion, or approximately 22 percent. Should inflation run at a higher rate, depreciation would supply a greater number of dollars, but a smaller percentage of total needs. Assuming that the historical 4.3 percent rate of return on net assets persists throughout the 15-year period, aggregate earnings should approximate $214 billion (6 percent inflation assumed). With cash dividends continuing at a rate of 75.5 percent of earnings, retained earnings should total about $52 billion, or slightly more than 8 percent of capital needs.

If projections for retained earnings and depreciation are reasonably accurate, internal funding will provide approximately $190 billion, or 30 percent of the funds required for capital spending, thus leaving a deficit of over $440 billion to be supplied by outside sources. While this is in line with funding sources in the early 1970s and early 1950s, it represents significant deterioration of the average over the past two decades. Indeed, the projections of Chapter 5 (Table 5.9) show a decreasing proportionate contribution by internal funds throughout the 1976-90 period, until the 1990s the industry will have to seek nearly 73 percent of total funds externally. With debt continuing at approximately 55 percent of capitalization, the industry would have to sell $170 billion of preferred and common stock over the 15-year interval. This represents over six times as much equity as was issued in the 25 years from 1948 to 1972. Should the utilities desire or be required to reduce the proportion of debt in their capital structures, the amount of equity issued would be correspondingly greater.

## CONCLUSIONS AND RECOMMENDATIONS

Reduced consumer demand for electricity, which followed the steeply higher prices of the early 1970s, offered utilities a small amount of breathing room in terms of capital expansion. However, the respite was considered by many to be only temporary.* The reduction in capital spending was more an industry reaction to an inability to finance expansion than a feeling that the demand for electricity would be significantly and permanently lower. In any case, the lag between the inception of new plants and their completion dates will conceal capacity shortages for up to a decade. In instances where construction has been delayed on partially completed plants, the shortages could be felt somewhat sooner.

It appears extremely unlikely that the industry will be able to finance the amount of capital expenditures estimated by *Electrical World* if internal sources contribute no more funds than have been estimated in this study. To expect common stockholders to absorb tens of billions of dollars in new equity issues, while at the same time many companies in the industry are earning less on equity capital than can be obtained by investors on long-term debt, seems overly optimistic. High rates of inflation and the resulting increase in long-term interest rates have made past earnings standards of the utilities obsolete. In many cases, companies in the industry have been fighting to revive profitability back to where it was years ago. In very few instances are they being allowed to earn a return which in today's economic climate is sufficient to facilitate adequate capital formation. While this type of regulation may be in the short-run interests of consumers, in that they pay less for electricity, it is less favorable when viewed from a long-run or even intermediate-term perspective. Paying a reduced price now, for an item that, as a result, may not be available in adequate quantities later, is a questionable goal.

The problem is more than a one-sided affair, however, for if capital requirements were reduced, internal flows would provide a larger percentage of financing. Depreciation, since it is a function of assets already acquired, would increase its proportionate contribution and retained earnings, which suffer from regulatory lag, would also provide more help. Although both depreciation and retained earnings would contribute fewer dollars, these dollars would represent a greater proportion of capital needs.

Keeping in mind that the financial health of the electric utilities is a function not only of past, present, and future earnings and cash flows, but also of prospective financial requirements, it is possible to develop some specific recommendations with respect to the industry. It is unfortunate that the major problems of the utilities—inflation and fuel prices—are variables over which they have little or no control. Rising prices inflate capital requirements, while at the

---

*The industry's actual capital expenditures in 1973 were nearly $2 billion less than had been forecast. Subsequent years through the mid-1970s should show a similar occurrence.

same time they diminish the relative contribution of internal funds and render traditional rates of return inadequate. Fuel price increases, even if they are passed on in fuel adjustment clauses, inhibit the utilities from recapturing cost increases in other areas.

1. *Alteration of Rate Structures*. Tariff schedules should be flattened in combination with an increased usage of peak-load pricing. For years utilities have used declining marginal costs as a justification for the decreasing block rates. With the present rate of inflation in capital costs, it becomes more difficult to accept this argument. Not only would a flattened rate structure more closely track long-run incremental costs, but the change would be in keeping with a national commitment to energy conservation. As a bonus to the industry, it would appear that both the public and many regulatory commissions would be less hostile to utility requests for tariff increases if these requests were combined with a change in the structure of rates.

The implementation of peak-load pricing would result in a smoothing of daily load variations, thereby improving load factors, and reduce the need for new capital expenditures to meet peak demand requirements. The two most frequently used arguments against this type of tariff system are that peak usage will merely shift from one period to another and that the cost of metering is too expensive in relation to the derived benefits. While the peak might possibly shift, it seems extremely doubtful that the new peak would be as high as that which existed prior to the change. In any case, rates could be altered once consumers adjusted to the initial change, so that further refinement could be achieved. While at one time the cost of metering was too expensive to justify its use on a widespread scale, recent improvements in metering technology, combined with changing cost conditions for the utilities, have reduced the validity of this argument.[7]

2. *An Increase in the Allowed Rate of Return*. With the increased returns available on alternative investments, it is foolhardy to expect investors to accept a continuation of past utility earnings standards. While the increased rates entailed in providing a higher return would have some effect upon the quantity of electricity demanded and thereby lower capital requirements, the primary consequence would be the improved ability of utilities to raise capital funds. Common stock would become more attractive to investors and the deterioration in interest coverage ratios would be reversed. In addition, an increase in earnings after dividends would provide a needed lift to internal funding. A 1974 report by the Federal Power Commission estimated that to increase the realized rate of return on common equity from 12 to 14 percent, the electric utilities would need to increase average consumer charges about 5 percent.[8] When combined with revamped tariff structures and peak-load pricing, the needed increase would be even less.

3. *Adoption of More Conservative Accounting Practices.* In order to maximize current earnings to shareholders many individual utilities use accounting methods which penalize cash flow and lend credence to the concern over the quality of reported earnings. To help remedy this, various accounting adjustments should be made including the normalizing of tax reductions from investment expenditures and the expensing of more items which are currently deferred.

4. *The Inclusion of Construction Work in Progress in the Rate Base.* While this proposal would have differing effects among individual companies, it would be most beneficial to those utilities which had the largest construction programs and, thus, the greatest need for capital funds. The replacement of the noncash item, allowance for funds during construction, with actual cash earnings would improve the quality of reported earnings and help restore investor confidence in utility equity and debt issues.

5. *Minimizing Regulatory Lag.* To minimize the effects of regulatory lag upon electric utilities, greater reliance on interim rate relief should be combined with the use of future, rather than historical, test periods. These two changes would help alleviate many of the financial problems associated with rapid inflation.

6. *Elimination of the Fuel Adjustment Charge.* Electric utilities are typically permitted to automatically pass through fuel price increases, but must apply for and wait through regulatory lag in order to recover capital cost increases. The result is a tendency to avoid capital intensive plant and equipment regardless of the fuel costs which will be incurred. The inefficient resource allocation this entails would be eliminated if all cost increases were put on an equal basis. The feasibility of this proposal is dependent upon implementation of the recommendations mentioned above.

7. *Subsidies to the Industry such as Federal Guarantees on Debt,*[9] *Elimination of Taxation on Cash Dividends, and Enactment of Larger Investment Tax Credits or Depreciation Allowances than Are Available to Other Industries Should Be Avoided.* There is no reason that taxpayers should be required to subsidize the consumers of electricity. In any case, increased tax credits and depreciation allowances would prove more helpful to utilities that are relatively healthy rather than to those which are financially weak. If the electric utilities are allowed to earn a fair return on their investment through proper tariff levels and rate structures the industry can achieve financial health without being subsidized.

## NOTES

1. U.S. Federal Power Commission, *Report of the Task Force on Utility Fuels Requirements*, August 1973, p. 37.

2. George P. Smith, "Electricity and the Environment: A Season of Discontent," *Federal Bar Journal* 33, no. 4 (Fall 1974): 271-82.

3. United Engineers and Constructors, Inc., U.S., Atomic Energy Commission Reports WASH-1082 and WASH-1230. See also, USAEC Reports WASH-1150 and NUS-531.

4. U.S. Atomic Energy Commission, *Power Plant Capital Costs: Current Trends and Sensitivity to Economic Parameters* (Washington: U.S. Government Printing Office, 1974), pp. 12-15.

5. U.S. Federal Power Commission, *Statistics of Privately Owned Electric Utilities in the United States* (Washington: U.S. Government Printing Office, various years).

6. See "24th Annual Electrical Industry Forecast," *Electrical World* 180, no. 6 (September 15, 1973): 53; and "25th Annual Electrical Industry Forecast," *Electrical World* 181, no. 6 (September 15, 1974): 57.

7. Edward Berlin, Charles Cicchetti, and William Gillen, *Perspective on Power* (Cambridge, Massachusetts: Ballinger Publishing Company, 1974), p. 45.

8. U.S. Federal Power Commission, "An Analysis of the Electric Utility Industry's Financial Requirements: 1975-79," (September 1974), p. 21.

9. See Murray L. Weidenbaum, "The Case Against Government Guarantees of Electric Utility Bonds," *Financial Management* 3, no. 3 (Autumn 1974): 24-30.

## TABLE A.1

Projected Annual Depreciation and Capital Requirements for Investor-Owned
Utilities at 4 and 5 Percent Inflation, 1976-90
(millions of dollars)

| Year | 4 Percent Inflation | | | 5 Percent Inflation | | |
|---|---|---|---|---|---|---|
| | Capital Requirements | Depreciation | Percent of Funds Provided by Depreciation | Capital Requirements | Depreciation | Percent of Funds Provided by Depreciation |
| 1976 | 14,985 | 4,310 | 28.8 | 15,262 | 4,322 | 28.3 |
| 1977 | 16,270 | 4,633 | 28.5 | 16,747 | 4,658 | 27.8 |
| 1978 | 17,437 | 4,979 | 28.5 | 18,793 | 5,040 | 26.8 |
| 1979 | 18,711 | 5,350 | 28.6 | 19,618 | 5,433 | 27.6 |
| 1980 | 21,322 | 5,781 | 27.1 | 22,626 | 5,897 | 26.0 |
| 1981 | 25,165 | 6,302 | 25.1 | 26,798 | 5,462 | 24.1 |
| 1982 | 28,785 | 6,909 | 24.0 | 31,055 | 7,126 | 22.9 |
| 1983 | 31,830 | 7,581 | 23.8 | 34,643 | 7,870 | 22.7 |
| 1984 | 34,589 | 8,311 | 24.0 | 38,071 | 8,685 | 22.8 |
| 1985 | 36,397 | 9,069 | 24.9 | 40,442 | 9,543 | 23.6 |
| 1986 | 41,512 | 9,945 | 23.9 | 46,568 | 10,543 | 22.6 |
| 1987 | 47,124 | 10,949 | 23.2 | 52,658 | 11,680 | 22.1 |
| 1988 | 52,672 | 12,075 | 22.9 | 60,529 | 12,999 | 21.5 |
| 1989 | 59,314 | 13,351 | 22.5 | 68,470 | 14,470 | 21.2 |
| 1990 | 66,166 | 14,777 | 22.3 | 77,117 | 16,187 | 20.9 |
| Total | 512,179 | 124,322 | 24.2 | 569,447 | 130,941 | 23.0 |

*Source*: Capital spending requirements computed from estimates by *Electrical World* 182, no. 6 (September 15, 1974): 57.

103

## TABLE A.2

### Projected Annual Depreciation and Capital Requirements for Investor-Owned Electric Utilities at 7 and 8 Percent Inflation, 1976-90
(millions of dollars)

| Year | 7 Percent Inflation | | | 8 Percent Inflation | | |
|---|---|---|---|---|---|---|
| | Capital Requirements | Depreciation | Percent of Funds Provided by Depreciation | Capital Requirements | Depreciation | Percent of Funds Provided by Depreciation |
| 1976 | 15,857 | 4,348 | 27.4 | 16,148 | 4,361 | 27.0 |
| 1977 | 17,716 | 4,709 | 26.6 | 18,220 | 4,735 | 25.9 |
| 1978 | 19,538 | 5,109 | 26.1 | 20,268 | 5,154 | 25.4 |
| 1979 | 21,571 | 5,554 | 25.7 | 22,586 | 5,625 | 24.9 |
| 1980 | 25,229 | 6,087 | 24.1 | 26.749 | 6,195 | 23.1 |
| 1981 | 30,588 | 6,748 | 22.1 | 32,645 | 6,909 | 21.2 |
| 1982 | 36,123 | 7,542 | 20.8 | 38,919 | 7,773 | 19.9 |
| 1983 | 41,112 | 8,448 | 20.5 | 44,714 | 8,771 | 19.6 |
| 1984 | 45,971 | 9,461 | 20.5 | 50,458 | 9,897 | 19.6 |
| 1985 | 49,783 | 10,550 | 21.2 | 55,152 | 11,118 | 20.1 |
| 1986 | 58,392 | 11,842 | 20.3 | 65,289 | 12,581 | 19.3 |
| 1987 | 68,187 | 13,363 | 19.6 | 76,779 | 14,655 | 19.0 |
| 1988 | 78,840 | 15,131 | 19.2 | 89,784 | 16,683 | 18.5 |
| 1989 | 90,865 | 17,175 | 18.9 | 104,467 | 19,053 | 18.2 |
| 1990 | 104,282 | 19,527 | 18.7 | 121,127 | 21,807 | 18.0 |
| Total | 704,124 | 145,594 | 20.6 | 783,225 | 155,317 | 19.8 |

*Source:* Capital spending requirements computed from estimates by *Electrical World* 182, no. 6 (September 15, 1974): 57.

## TABLE B.1

### Projected Net Profits and Retained Earnings with 4 Percent Inflation for Investor-Owned Electric Utilities, 1976-90 (millions of dollars)

| Year | Return on Net Assets (percent) | | | | | | |
|---|---|---|---|---|---|---|---|
| | 4.0 | 4.1 | 4.2 | 4.3 | 4.4 | 4.5 | 4.6 |
| *Net Profits* | | | | | | | |
| 1976 | 6,213 | 6,368 | 6,524 | 6,679 | 6,834 | 6,990 | 7,145 |
| 1977 | 6,674 | 6,846 | 7,013 | 7,179 | 7,346 | 7,513 | 7,680 |
| 1978 | 7,177 | 7,356 | 7,536 | 7,715 | 7,895 | 8,074 | 8,253 |
| 1979 | 7,711 | 7,904 | 8,097 | 8,290 | 8,482 | 8,675 | 8,868 |
| 1980 | 8,333 | 8,541 | 8,750 | 8,958 | 9,166 | 9,375 | 9,583 |
| 1981 | 9,084 | 9,311 | 9,538 | 9,765 | 9,992 | 10,219 | 10,446 |
| 1982 | 9,959 | 10,208 | 10,456 | 10,705 | 10,954 | 11,203 | 11,452 |
| 1983 | 10,929 | 11,202 | 11,475 | 11,748 | 12,021 | 12,295 | 12,568 |
| 1984 | 11,980 | 12,279 | 12,579 | 12,878 | 13,178 | 13,477 | 13,777 |
| 1985 | 13,072 | 13,400 | 13,726 | 14,053 | 14,380 | 14,707 | 15,034 |
| 1986 | 14,335 | 14,694 | 15,052 | 15,411 | 15,769 | 16,127 | 16,486 |
| 1987 | 15,782 | 16,177 | 16,572 | 16,966 | 17,361 | 17,755 | 18,150 |
| 1988 | 17,406 | 17,841 | 18,277 | 18,712 | 19,147 | 19,582 | 20,017 |
| 1989 | 19,245 | 19,726 | 20,207 | 20,688 | 21,169 | 21,650 | 22,132 |
| 1990 | 21,300 | 21,833 | 22,365 | 22,989 | 22,430 | 23,963 | 24,495 |
| Total | 179,205 | 183,686 | 188,167 | 192,645 | 197,124 | 201,605 | 206,086 |
| *Retained Earnings* | | | | | | | |
| 1976 | 1,522 | 1,560 | 1,560 | 1,636 | 1,674 | 1,713 | 1,751 |
| 1977 | 1,636 | 1,677 | 1,718 | 1,759 | 1,800 | 1,841 | 1,882 |
| 1978 | 1,758 | 1,802 | 1,846 | 1,890 | 1,934 | 1,978 | 2,022 |
| 1979 | 1,889 | 1,936 | 1,984 | 2,031 | 2,078 | 2,125 | 2,173 |
| 1980 | 2,042 | 2,092 | 2,144 | 2,195 | 2,246 | 2,297 | 2,348 |
| 1981 | 2,226 | 2,281 | 2,377 | 2,392 | 2,448 | 2,504 | 2,559 |
| 1982 | 2,440 | 2,501 | 2,562 | 2,623 | 2,684 | 2,745 | 2,806 |
| 1983 | 2,678 | 2,744 | 2,811 | 2,878 | 2,945 | 3,012 | 3,079 |
| 1984 | 2,935 | 3,008 | 3,082 | 3,155 | 3,229 | 3,302 | 3,375 |
| 1985 | 3,203 | 3,283 | 3,363 | 3,443 | 3,523 | 3,603 | 3,683 |
| 1986 | 3,512 | 3,600 | 3,688 | 3,776 | 3,863 | 3,951 | 4,039 |
| 1987 | 3,867 | 3,963 | 4,060 | 4,157 | 4,253 | 4,350 | 4,447 |
| 1988 | 4,264 | 4,371 | 4,478 | 4,584 | 4,691 | 4,798 | 4,904 |
| 1989 | 4,715 | 4,833 | 4,951 | 5,069 | 5,186 | 5,304 | 5,422 |
| 1990 | 5,218 | 5,349 | 5,479 | 5,610 | 5,740 | 5,871 | 6,001 |
| Total | 43,905 | 45,000 | 46,141 | 47,198 | 48,294 | 49,394 | 50,491 |

*Source*: Compiled by author.

## TABLE B.2

### Projected Net Profits and Retained Earnings with 5 Percent Inflation for Investor-Owned Electric Utilities, 1976-90 (millions of dollars)

| Year | Return on Net Assets (percent) | | | | | | |
|------|------|------|------|------|------|------|------|
| | 4.0 | 4.1 | 4.2 | 4.3 | 4.4 | 4.5 | 4.6 |
| *Net Profits* | | | | | | | |
| 1976 | 6,231 | 6,387 | 6,543 | 6,699 | 6,854 | 7,010 | 7,166 |
| 1977 | 6,715 | 6,883 | 7,051 | 7,218 | 7,387 | 7,554 | 7,722 |
| 1978 | 7,239 | 7,420 | 7,601 | 7,782 | 7,963 | 8,144 | 8,325 |
| 1979 | 7,808 | 8,003 | 8,198 | 8,393 | 8,589 | 8,784 | 8,979 |
| 1980 | 8,477 | 8,689 | 8,901 | 9,113 | 9,325 | 9,537 | 9,749 |
| 1981 | 9,301 | 9,533 | 9,766 | 9,998 | 10,231 | 10,464 | 10,696 |
| 1982 | 10,255 | 10,512 | 10,768 | 11,024 | 11,281 | 11,537 | 11,793 |
| 1983 | 11,333 | 11,616 | 11,900 | 12,183 | 12,466 | 12,749 | 13,033 |
| 1984 | 12,515 | 12,826 | 13,140 | 13,453 | 13,766 | 14,079 | 14,392 |
| 1985 | 13,758 | 14,102 | 14,446 | 14,790 | 15,134 | 15,478 | 15,822 |
| 1986 | 15,210 | 15,590 | 15,970 | 16,351 | 16,731 | 17,111 | 17,491 |
| 1987 | 16,890 | 17,312 | 17,734 | 18,157 | 18,579 | 19,001 | 19,424 |
| 1988 | 18,804 | 19,274 | 19,744 | 20,214 | 20,684 | 21,155 | 21,625 |
| 1989 | 20,987 | 21,511 | 22,036 | 22,561 | 23,085 | 23,610 | 24,135 |
| 1990 | 23,454 | 24,040 | 24,627 | 25,213 | 25,799 | 26,386 | 26,972 |
| Total | 188,977 | 193,698 | 198,425 | 203,149 | 207,873 | 212,599 | 217,324 |
| *Retained Earnings* | | | | | | | |
| 1976 | 1,527 | 1,565 | 1,603 | 1,641 | 1,679 | 1,717 | 1,756 |
| 1977 | 1,645 | 1,686 | 1,719 | 1,768 | 1,810 | 1,851 | 1,892 |
| 1978 | 1,774 | 1,818 | 1,862 | 1,907 | 1,951 | 1,995 | 2,040 |
| 1979 | 1,913 | 1,961 | 2,009 | 2,056 | 2,104 | 2,152 | 2,200 |
| 1980 | 2,077 | 2,129 | 2,181 | 2,233 | 2,285 | 2,337 | 2,389 |
| 1981 | 2,279 | 2,336 | 2,393 | 2,450 | 2,507 | 2,564 | 2,621 |
| 1982 | 2,512 | 2,575 | 2,638 | 2,701 | 2,764 | 2,827 | 2,889 |
| 1983 | 2,777 | 2,846 | 2,916 | 2,985 | 3,054 | 3,124 | 3,193 |
| 1984 | 3,066 | 3,142 | 3,219 | 3,296 | 3,373 | 3,449 | 3,526 |
| 1985 | 3,371 | 3,455 | 3,539 | 3,624 | 3,708 | 3,792 | 3,876 |
| 1986 | 3,726 | 3,820 | 3,913 | 4,005 | 4,099 | 4,192 | 4,285 |
| 1987 | 4,138 | 4,241 | 4,345 | 4,448 | 4,552 | 4,655 | 4,759 |
| 1988 | 4,607 | 4,722 | 4,837 | 4,952 | 5,068 | 5,183 | 5,298 |
| 1989 | 5,142 | 5,270 | 5,399 | 5,527 | 5,656 | 5,784 | 5,913 |
| 1990 | 5,746 | 5,890 | 6,034 | 6,177 | 6,321 | 6,465 | 6,608 |
| Total | 46,300 | 47,456 | 48,607 | 49,770 | 50,931 | 52,087 | 53,245 |

*Source*: Compiled by author.

# TABLE B.3

## Projected Net Profits and Retained Earnings with 6 Percent Inflation for Investor-Owned Electric Utilities, 1976-90
### (millions of dollars)

| | Return on Net Assets (percent) | | | | | | |
|---|---|---|---|---|---|---|---|
| Year | 4.0 | 4.1 | 4.2 | 4.3 | 4.4 | 4.5 | 4.6 |
| *Net Profits* | | | | | | | |
| 1976 | 6,249 | 6,406 | 6,562 | 6,718 | 6,874 | 7,031 | 7,187 |
| 1977 | 6,751 | 6,920 | 7,088 | 7,257 | 7,426 | 7,595 | 7,764 |
| 1978 | 7,301 | 7,483 | 7,666 | 7,848 | 8,031 | 7,213 | 8,396 |
| 1979 | 7,904 | 8,102 | 8,300 | 8,497 | 8,695 | 8,892 | 9,090 |
| 1980 | 8,622 | 8,837 | 9,053 | 9,268 | 9,484 | 9,700 | 9,915 |
| 1981 | 9,504 | 9,741 | 9,979 | 10,217 | 10,454 | 10,692 | 10,929 |
| 1982 | 10,552 | 10,815 | 11,079 | 11,343 | 11,607 | 11,871 | 12,134 |
| 1983 | 11,737 | 12,031 | 12,324 | 12,617 | 12,911 | 13,204 | 13,498 |
| 1984 | 13,049 | 13,376 | 13,702 | 14,028 | 14,354 | 14,680 | 15,007 |
| 1985 | 14,444 | 14,805 | 15,166 | 15,527 | 15,888 | 16,250 | 16,611 |
| 1986 | 16,084 | 16,487 | 16,889 | 17,291 | 17,693 | 18,085 | 18,497 |
| 1987 | 17,997 | 18,447 | 18,897 | 19,347 | 19,797 | 20,247 | 20,697 |
| 1988 | 20,202 | 20,707 | 21,212 | 21,717 | 22,222 | 22,727 | 23,232 |
| 1989 | 22,729 | 23,297 | 23,865 | 24,433 | 25,002 | 25,570 | 26,138 |
| 1990 | 25,607 | 26,247 | 26,888 | 27,528 | 28,168 | 28,808 | 29,448 |
| Total | 198,732 | 203,701 | 208,670 | 213,636 | 211,926 | 223,575 | 228,543 |
| *Retained Earnings* | | | | | | | |
| 1976 | 1,531 | 1,570 | 1,608 | 1,646 | 1,684 | 1,723 | 1,761 |
| 1977 | 1,654 | 1,695 | 1,737 | 1,778 | 1,819 | 1,861 | 1,903 |
| 1978 | 1,789 | 1,833 | 1,878 | 1,923 | 1,968 | 2,012 | 2,057 |
| 1979 | 1,937 | 1,985 | 2,034 | 2,082 | 2,130 | 2,179 | 2,227 |
| 1980 | 2,112 | 2,165 | 2,218 | 1,271 | 2,324 | 2,376 | 2,429 |
| 1981 | 2,329 | 2,387 | 2,445 | 2,503 | 2,561 | 2,620 | 2,678 |
| 1982 | 2,585 | 2,650 | 2,714 | 2,779 | 2,844 | 2,908 | 2,973 |
| 1983 | 2,876 | 2,948 | 3,019 | 3,091 | 3,163 | 3,235 | 3,307 |
| 1984 | 3,197 | 3,277 | 3,357 | 3,437 | 3,517 | 3,597 | 3,677 |
| 1985 | 3,539 | 3,627 | 3,716 | 3,804 | 3,893 | 3,981 | 4,070 |
| 1986 | 3,941 | 4,039 | 4,138 | 4,236 | 4,335 | 4,433 | 4,532 |
| 1987 | 4,409 | 4,502 | 4,630 | 4,740 | 4,850 | 4,961 | 5,071 |
| 1988 | 4,950 | 5,073 | 5,197 | 5,321 | 5,444 | 5,568 | 5,692 |
| 1989 | 5,569 | 5,708 | 5,847 | 5,986 | 6,126 | 6,265 | 6,406 |
| 1990 | 6,274 | 6,431 | 6,588 | 6,744 | 6,901 | 7,058 | 7,215 |
| Total | 48,692 | 49,908 | 51,126 | 52,341 | 53,559 | 54,777 | 55,998 |

*Source*: Compiled by author.

# TABLE B.4

## Projected Net Profits and Retained Earnings with 7 Percent Inflation for Investor-Owned Electric Utilities, 1976-90 (millions of dollars)

| Year | Return on Net Assets (percent) | | | | | | |
|------|-------|-------|-------|-------|-------|-------|-------|
|      | 4.0   | 4.1   | 4.2   | 4.3   | 4.4   | 4.5   | 4.6   |
| *Net Profits* | | | | | | | |
| 1976 | 6,268 | 6,424 | 6,581 | 6,738 | 6,894 | 7,051 | 7,208 |
| 1977 | 6,787 | 6,957 | 7,127 | 7,296 | 7,466 | 7,636 | 7,805 |
| 1978 | 7,363 | 7,547 | 7,731 | 7,915 | 8,099 | 8,283 | 8,467 |
| 1979 | 8,001 | 8,201 | 8,401 | 8,601 | 8,801 | 8,001 | 9,201 |
| 1980 | 8,766 | 8,985 | 9,204 | 9,424 | 9,643 | 9,862 | 10,081 |
| 1981 | 9,714 | 9,957 | 10,200 | 10,443 | 10,685 | 10,928 | 11,171 |
| 1982 | 10,848 | 11,119 | 11,391 | 11,662 | 11,933 | 12,204 | 12,475 |
| 1983 | 12,142 | 12,445 | 12,749 | 13,052 | 13,356 | 13,659 | 13,963 |
| 1984 | 13,584 | 13,924 | 14,263 | 14,603 | 14,943 | 15,282 | 15,622 |
| 1985 | 15,130 | 15,508 | 15,886 | 16,264 | 16,643 | 17,021 | 17,399 |
| 1986 | 16,960 | 17,384 | 17,808 | 18,232 | 18,656 | 19,080 | 19,504 |
| 1987 | 19,105 | 19,583 | 20,060 | 20,538 | 21,016 | 21,493 | 21,971 |
| 1988 | 21,599 | 22,139 | 22,679 | 23,219 | 23,759 | 24,299 | 24,839 |
| 1989 | 24,471 | 25,082 | 25,694 | 26,306 | 26,918 | 27,529 | 28,141 |
| 1990 | 27,761 | 28,455 | 29,149 | 29,843 | 30,537 | 31,231 | 31,925 |
| Total | 208,499 | 213,710 | 218,923 | 224,136 | 229,349 | 234,559 | 239,772 |
| *Retained Earnings* | | | | | | | |
| 1976 | 1,536 | 1,574 | 1,612 | 1,651 | 1,689 | 1,727 | 1,766 |
| 1977 | 1,663 | 1,704 | 1,746 | 1,788 | 1,829 | 1,871 | 1,912 |
| 1978 | 1,804 | 1,849 | 1,894 | 1,939 | 1,984 | 2,029 | 2,074 |
| 1979 | 1,960 | 2,009 | 2,058 | 2,107 | 2,156 | 2,205 | 2,254 |
| 1980 | 2,148 | 2,201 | 2,255 | 2,309 | 2,363 | 2,316 | 2,470 |
| 1981 | 2,380 | 2,439 | 2,499 | 2,559 | 2,618 | 2,677 | 2,737 |
| 1982 | 2,658 | 2,724 | 2,791 | 2,857 | 2,924 | 2,990 | 3,056 |
| 1983 | 2,975 | 3,049 | 3,124 | 3,198 | 3,272 | 3,346 | 3,421 |
| 1984 | 3,328 | 3,411 | 3,494 | 3,578 | 3,661 | 3,744 | 3,827 |
| 1985 | 3,707 | 3,799 | 3,892 | 3,985 | 4,078 | 4,170 | 4,263 |
| 1986 | 4,155 | 4,259 | 4,363 | 4,467 | 4,571 | 4,675 | 4,778 |
| 1987 | 4,681 | 4,798 | 4,915 | 5,032 | 5,148 | 5,266 | 5,383 |
| 1988 | 5,292 | 5,424 | 5,556 | 5,689 | 5,821 | 5,953 | 6,086 |
| 1989 | 5,995 | 6,145 | 6,295 | 6,445 | 6,595 | 6,745 | 6,895 |
| 1990 | 6,801 | 6,971 | 7,142 | 7,312 | 7,482 | 7,652 | 7,822 |
| Total | 51,082 | 52,359 | 53,636 | 54,913 | 56,191 | 57,467 | 58,744 |

*Source*: Compiled by author.

# TABLE B.5

## Projected Net Profits and Retained Earnings with 8 Percent Inflation for Investor-Owned Electric Utilities, 1976-90 (millions of dollars)

| Year | Return on Net Assets (percent) | | | | | | |
|------|------|------|------|------|------|------|------|
|      | 4.0 | 4.1 | 4.2 | 4.3 | 4.4 | 4.5 | 4.6 |
| *Net Profits* | | | | | | | |
| 1976 | 6,286 | 6,443 | 6,600 | 6,757 | 6,914 | 7,071 | 7,229 |
| 1977 | 6,824 | 6,994 | 7,165 | 7,335 | 7,506 | 7,676 | 7,847 |
| 1978 | 7,425 | 7,610 | 7,796 | 7,981 | 8,167 | 8,353 | 8,538 |
| 1979 | 8,097 | 8,300 | 8,502 | 8,705 | 8,907 | 9,109 | 9,312 |
| 1980 | 8,911 | 9,133 | 9,356 | 9,578 | 9,802 | 10,024 | 10,247 |
| 1981 | 9,924 | 10,172 | 10,420 | 10,669 | 10,669 | 10,917 | 11,413 |
| 1982 | 11,145 | 11,423 | 11,702 | 11,981 | 12,259 | 12,538 | 12,816 |
| 1983 | 12,546 | 12,859 | 13,173 | 13,487 | 13,800 | 14,114 | 14,428 |
| 1984 | 14,119 | 14,472 | 14,825 | 15,178 | 15,531 | 15,884 | 16,237 |
| 1985 | 15,815 | 16,211 | 16,606 | 17,002 | 17,397 | 17,792 | 18,188 |
| 1986 | 17,835 | 18,281 | 18,726 | 19,172 | 19,618 | 20,064 | 20,510 |
| 1987 | 20,213 | 20,718 | 21,223 | 21,729 | 22,234 | 22,739 | 23,244 |
| 1988 | 22,997 | 23,572 | 24,147 | 24,722 | 25,297 | 25,872 | 26,447 |
| 1989 | 26,213 | 26,868 | 27,523 | 28,179 | 28,834 | 29,489 | 30,144 |
| 1990 | 29,914 | 30,662 | 31,410 | 32,158 | 32,906 | 33,653 | 34,401 |
| Total | 218,264 | 223,718 | 229,174 | 234,633 | 240,089 | 205,543 | 251,001 |
| *Retained Earnings* | | | | | | | |
| 1976 | 1,540 | 1,579 | 1,617 | 1,655 | 1,694 | 1,732 | 1,771 |
| 1977 | 1,672 | 1,714 | 1,755 | 1,797 | 1,839 | 1,881 | 1,923 |
| 1978 | 1,819 | 1,864 | 1,910 | 1,955 | 2,001 | 2,046 | 2,092 |
| 1979 | 1,984 | 2,034 | 2,083 | 2,133 | 2,182 | 2,232 | 2,281 |
| 1980 | 2,183 | 2,238 | 2,292 | 2,347 | 2,401 | 2,456 | 2,511 |
| 1981 | 2,431 | 2,492 | 2,553 | 2,614 | 2,675 | 2,735 | 2,796 |
| 1982 | 2,731 | 2,799 | 2,867 | 2,935 | 3,003 | 3,072 | 3,140 |
| 1983 | 3,074 | 3,150 | 3,227 | 3,304 | 3,381 | 3,458 | 3,535 |
| 1984 | 3,459 | 3,546 | 3,632 | 3,719 | 3,805 | 3,892 | 3,978 |
| 1985 | 3,875 | 3,972 | 4,068 | 4,165 | 4,262 | 4,359 | 4,456 |
| 1986 | 4,370 | 4,479 | 4,588 | 4,697 | 4,806 | 4,916 | 5,025 |
| 1987 | 4,952 | 5,076 | 5,200 | 5,324 | 5,447 | 5,571 | 5,695 |
| 1988 | 5,634 | 5,775 | 5,916 | 6,057 | 6,198 | 6,339 | 6,480 |
| 1989 | 6,422 | 6,582 | 6,743 | 6,904 | 7,064 | 7,225 | 7,385 |
| 1990 | 7,329 | 7,512 | 7,695 | 7,879 | 8,062 | 8,245 | 8,428 |
| Total | 53,475 | 54,811 | 56,148 | 57,485 | 458,822 | 60,158 | 61,495 |

*Source*: Compiled by author.

# BOOKS

Berlin, Edward, Charles J. Cicchetti, and William J. Gillen. *Perspective on Power*. Cambridge, Massachusetts: Ballinger Publishing Co., 1974.

Bosworth, Barry, James S. Duesenberry, and Andrew S. Carron. *Capital Needs in the Seventies*. Washington: Brookings Institution, 1975.

Brannon, Gerald M. *Energy Taxes and Subsidies*. Cambridge, Massachusetts: Ballinger Publishing Co., 1974.

Breyer, Stephen G., and Paul W. MacAvoy. *Energy Regulation by the Federal Power Commission*. Washington: Brookings Institution, 1974.

Cicchetti, Charles J., and John Jurewitz, eds. *Studies in Electric Utility Regulation*. Cambridge, Massachusetts: Ballinger Publishing Co., 1974.

Duchesneau, Thomas. *Competition in the U.S. Energy Industry*. Cambridge, Massachusetts: Ballinger Publishing Co., 1974.

Dupree, Walter G., and James A. West. *United States Energy Through the Year 2000*. Washington: U.S. Government Printing Office, 1972.

Edison Electric Institute. *Statistical Year Book of the Electric Utility Industry*. New York: Edison Electric Institute, various years.

Farris, Martin, and Roy Sampson. *Public Utilities*. Boston: Houghton Mifflin, 1973.

Fisher, F.M., and C.A. Kaysen. *A Study in Econometrics: The Demand for Electricity in the United States*. Amsterdam: North Holland Publishing Co., 1962.

Fisher, John C. *Energy Crisis in Perspective*. New York: John Wiley and Sons, 1974.

Gordon, Myron J. *The Cost of Capital to a Public Utility*. Lansing: Michigan State University Press, 1974.

Hass, Jerome E., Edward J. Mitchell, and Bernell K. Stone. *Financing the Energy Industry*. Cambridge, Massachusetts: Ballinger Publishing Co., 1974.

MacAvoy, P.W. *Economic Strategy for Developing Nuclear Breeder Reactors*. Cambridge, Massachusetts: MIT Press, 1969.

National Association of Regulatory Utility Commissioners. *The Measurement of Electric Utility Efficiency*. Washington: National Association of Regulatory Utility Commissioners, 1975.

Olson, Charles E. *Cost Considerations for Efficient Electricity Supply*. Lansing: Michigan State University Press, 1970.

Rabwowitz, Alan. *Municipal Bond Finance and Administration*. New York: Wiley-Interscience, 1969.

Ray, Marvin E. *The Environmental Crisis and Corporate Debt Capacity*. Lexington, Massachusetts: D.C. Heath and Co., 1974.

Scott, David L. *Pollution in the Electric Power Industry: Its Control and Costs*. Lexington, Massachusetts: D.C. Heath and Co., 1973.

Turvey, Ralph. *Optimal Pricing and Investment in Electricity Supply*. Cambridge, Massachusetts: MIT Press, 1968.

United Engineers and Constructors, Inc. *1000 MWE Central Station Power Plant Investment Cost Study*. U.S. Atomic Energy Commission Report, Wash-1230. Washington: U.S. Government Printing Office, 1974.

U.S. Atomic Energy Commission. *Power Plant Capital Costs: Current Trends and Sensitivity to Economic Parameters*. Washington: U.S. Government Printing Office, 1974.

U.S. Department of Agriculture, Rural Electrification Administration. *Annual Statistical Report: REA Bulletin 1-1*. Washington: U.S. Government Printing Office, various years.

——————. *Rural Lines: The Story of Cooperative Rural Electrification*. Washington: U.S. Government Printing Office, 1973.

U.S. Environmental Protection Agency. *The Economic and Environmental Benefits from Improving Electrical Rate Structures*. Washington: U.S. Government Printing Office, 1974.

U.S. Federal Power Commission. *Annual Report*. Washington: U.S. Government Printing Office, various years.

——————. *1970 National Power Survey*. Washington: U.S. Government Printing Office, 1971.

——————. *Statistics of Privately Owned Electric Utilities in the United States*. Washington: U.S. Government Printing Office, various years.

——————. *Statistics of Publicly Owned Electric Utilities in the United States*. Washington: U.S. Government Printing Office, various years.

——————. *Steam-Electric Plant Construction Cost and Annual Production Expenses*. Washington: U.S. Government Printing Office, various years.

——————. *Typical Electric Bills*. Washington: U.S. Government Printing Office, various years.

Weidenbaum, Murray L. *Financing the Electric Utility Industry.* New York: Edison Electric
    Institute, 1974.


## Articles

Anderson, Daniel C., and Hans-Peter Fetzer. "Detail on Electric Utility Plant Investment by
    FPC Accounts," *Public Utilities Fortnightly* 94 (August 1, 1974): 28-31.

Bailey, Elizabeth E. "Peak Load Pricing under Regulatory Constraint," *Journal of Political
    Economy* 80 (July/August 1972): 662-79.

Bailey, Elizabeth E., and John C. Malone. "Resource Allocation and the Regulated Firm."
    *Bell Journal of Economics and Management Science* (Spring 1970): 129-42.

Barkwill, Albert C. "The Single Payment Bond: An Innovative Financing Technique,"
    *Public Utilities Fortnightly* 93 (May 9, 1974): 31-35.

Baxter, R.E., and R. Rees. "Analysis of the Industrial Demand for Electricity," *Economic
    Journal* 78 (June 1968): 227-98.

Beaty, H. Wayne. "9th Annual T & D Construction Survey," *Electrical World* 182 (Septem-
    ber 1, 1974): 41-48.

Boggis, J.G. "Innovations in Domestic Tariff Metering," *Electricity* 19 (September/October
    1966): 241-44.

Brigham, Eugene F., and Myron J. Gordon. "Leverage, Dividend Policy and the Cost of
    Capital," *Journal of Finance* 23 (March 1968): 85-103.

Brophy, Theodore F. "The Utility Problem of Regulatory Lag," *Public Utilities Fortnightly*
    95 (January 30, 1975): 21-27.

Cargill, T.E., and T.A. Meyer. "Estimating the Demand for Electricity by Time of Day,"
    *Applied Economics* 3 (1971): 233-46.

Cicchetti, Charles J. "The Design of Electricity Tariffs," *Public Utilities Fortnightly* 94
    (August 28, 1968): 25-33.

DeSalvia, Donald N. "An Application of Peak Load Pricing," *Journal of Business* 42 (Octo-
    ber 1969): 458-76.

Elton, Edwin J., and Martin J. Gruber. "Valuation and the Cost of Capital for Regulated
    Industries," *Journal of Finance* 26 (June 1971): 661-70.

Gilbert, William A., and Richard V. DeGrasse. "Prospects for Electric Utility Load Manage-
    ment," *Public Utilities Fortnightly* 96 (August 28, 1975): 15-19.

Griffin, James M. "The Effects of Higher Prices on Electricity Consumption," *Bell Journal of Economics and Management Science* 5 (Autumn 1974): 515-39.

Halm, David A. "Stepping Up the Pace in Financing," *Public Utilities Fortnightly* 96 (September 27, 1975): 30-33.

Higgins, Robert C. "Growth, Dividend Policy and Capital Costs in the Electric Utility Industry," *Journal of Finance* 29 (September 1974): 1189-1201.

Huff, Barry W. "Financing with Industrial Revenue Bonds," *Public Utilities Fortnightly* 96 (July 3, 1975): 32-35.

Jaffee, Bruce L. "Future Changes in Electric Utility Rate Structures," *Public Utilities Fortnightly* 95 (April 10, 1975): 25-30.

Jones, Douglas N. "Conservation and Utility Earnings: A Policy Predicament," *Public Utilities Fortnightly* 93 (April 25, 1974): 25-30.

Kafoglis, Milton, and Charles Needy. "Spread in Electric Utility Rate Structures," *Bell Journal of Economics and Management Science* 6 (Spring 1975): 377-87.

Kendrick, John W. "Efficiency Incentives and Cost Factors in Public Utility Automatic Revenue Adjustment Clauses," *Bell Journal of Economics and Management Science* 6 (Spring 1975): 299-313.

Kintzele, Philip L. "Leasing in the Electric Utility Industry and How to Account for It," *Public Utilities Fortnightly* 93 (March 28, 1974): 27-31.

Lerner, Eugene M. "On Utility Financing," *Public Utilities Fortnightly* 95 (May 8, 1975): 30-34.

Manus, Peter C., and Charles F. Phillips. "Earnings Erosion During Inflation," *Public Utilities Fortnightly* 95 (May 8, 1975): 17-22.

Mayo, Herbert B. "Savings from Dividend Reinvestment Plans," *Public Utilities Fortnightly* 94 (September 12, 1974): 36-40.

McDiarmid, Fergus J. "The Rise and Decline of Electric Utility Credit," *Public Utilities Fortnightly* 95 (June 19, 1975): 19-22.

Merrill, Eugene S. "Investment Quality of Utility Bonds," *Public Utilities Fortnightly* 95 (February 27, 1975): 17-25.

Militello, Philip G. "Concepts in Demand Control," *Public Utilities Fortnightly* 96 (August 14, 1975): 29-34.

Miller, Merton, and Franco Modignani. "Some Estimates of the Cost of Capital to the Electric Utility Industry, 1954-57," *American Economic Review* 56 (June 1966): 333-91.

Phelps, George E. "That Bothersome Construction Interest Allowance," *Public Utilities Fortnightly* 93 (January 31, 1974): 21-27.

Rakes, G.K. "Risk Factors Affecting Power Company Securities," *Public Utilities Fortnightly* 96 (July 31, 1975): 17-21.

Robichek, Alexander A., Robert C. Higgins, and Michael Kinsman. "The Effect of Leverage on the Cost of Equity Capital of Electric Utility Firms," *Journal of Finance* 28 (May 1973): 353-67.

Rosen, Herman G. "Utility Financing Problems and National Energy Policy," *Public Utilities Fortnightly* 94 (September 12, 1974): 19-30.

Rosenberg, William G. "Kilowatts and Capital: The Real Energy Crisis," *Public Utilities Fortnightly* 95 (February 27, 1975): 26-29.

Rydbeck, Vernon A. "$R_x$ for Utility Financial Vitality," *Public Utilities Fortnightly* 96 (August 14, 1975): 17-21.

Seitz, W.D. "Productive Efficiency in the Steam Electric Generating Industry," *Journal of Political Economy* 79 (July/August 1971): 878-86.

Shaw, Donald H. "Erosion of Utility Common Stock Dividends," *Public Utilities Fortnightly* 93 (May 23, 1974): 26-30.

Steiner, P.O. "Peak Loads and Efficient Pricing," *Quarterly Journal of Economics* 71 (November 1957): 585-610.

Stevenson, Richard A. "Utilities Issuing Warrants: Rationale and Evaluation," *Public Utilities Fortnightly* 93 (April 1974): 26-30.

Stratton, William R. "Whither Utility Financing," *Public Utilities Fortnightly* 94 (October 10, 1974): 23-26.

Tatham, Charles. "Interest Coverage During Construction and Price-Earnings Ratios," *Public Utilities Fortnightly* 92 (September 27, 1973): 32-36.

Taylor, Lester D. "The Demand for Electricity: A Survey," *Bell Journal of Economics and Management Science* 6 (Spring 1975): 74-110.

Thomas, Briam C. "Test Metering Supports Rate Studies," *Electric World* 182 (August 1, 1974): 62-64.

Thornton, John V. "Restoring Investor Confidence in the Utility Industry," *Public Utilities Fortnightly* 94 (October 24, 1974): 34-37.

Turvey, Ralph. "Peak Load Pricing," *Journal of Political Economy* 76 (February 1968): 107-13.

"25th Annual Electrical Industry Forecast," *Electrical World* 182 (September 15, 1974): 43-58.

"24th Annual Electrical Industry Forecast," *Electrical World* 180 (September 15, 1973): 45-54.

Vickrey, William S. "Responsive Pricing of Public Utility Services," *Bell Journal of Economics and Management Sciences* 2 (Spring 1971): 337-46.

Weidenbaum, Murray L. "The Case Against Government Guarantees of Electrical Utility Bonds," *Financial Management* 3 (Autumn 1974): 24-30.

------. "Future Capital Requirements of the Electric Utility Industry, 1974-80," *Public Utilities Fortnightly* 95 (January 30, 1975): 15-20.

West, David A., and Arthur A. Eubank. "Automatic Cost of Capital Model," *Public Utilities Fortnightly* 95 (May 22, 1975): 27-32.

Wilder, Ronald P., and Stanley R. Stansell. "Determinants of Research and Development Activity by Electric Utilities," *Bell Journal of Economics and Management Science* 5 (Autumn 1974): 646-50.

Wilson, J.W. "Residential Demand for Electricity," *Quarterly Review of Economics and Business* 11 (Spring 1971): 7-22.

## Public Documents

U.S. Congress, House, Committee on Banking, Currency, and Housing. *Economics of Energy and Natural Resource Pricing.* Committee Print. 94th Cong., 1st Sess., 1975.

------. *Hearings on Energy Security and the Domestic Economy: Impact on Prices, Employment, and Consumption.* 93rd Cong., 2nd Sess., 1974.

U.S. Congress, House, Committee on Government Operations. *Hearings on Power Rate Increases (Bureau of Reclamation, Central Valley Project, California).* 93rd Cong., 2nd Sess., 1974.

U.S. Congress, House, Committee on Interior and Insular Affairs, Subcommittee on Environment. *Hearings on National Energy Research.* 93rd Cong., 1st and 2nd Sess., 1973 and 1974.

------. *Hearings on Review of Electric Power Rate Increases.* 93rd Cong., 2nd Sess., 1974.

U.S. Congress, House, Committee on Interstate and Foreign Commerce. *Hearings on Presidential Energy Program* 94th Cong., 1st Sess., 1975.

U.S. Congress, House, Committee on Public Works and Transportation. *TVA Bonding Authority.* Committee Report on H.R. 9472. 94th Cong., 1st Sess., 1975.

U.S. Congress, House, Committee on Science and Astronautics. *Inventory of Current Energy Research and Development.* Committee Print. 93rd Cong., 2nd Sess., 1974.

U.S. Congress, House, Committee on Science and Astronautics, Subcommittee on Energy. *Hearings on Research, Development, and the Energy Crisis.* 93rd Cong., 1st Sess., 1973.

U.S. Congress, House, Committee on Science and Technology. *Energy Facts II.* Committee Print. Washington: U.S. Government Printing Office, 1975.

U.S. Congress, House, Committee on Ways and Means. *Alternatives for Consideration in an Energy Program.* Committee Print. 94th Cong., 1st Sess., 1975.

——————. *Background Readings on Energy Policy* 94th Cong., 1st Sess., 1975.

——————. *Energy Crisis and Proposed Solutions.* Committee Print. 94th Cong., 1st Sess., 1975.

——————. *Summary of Energy Facts and Issues.* 94th Cong., 1st Sess., 1975.

U.S. Congress, House, Subcommittee on Communications and Power. *Hearings on Power Plant Siting and Environmental Protection.* 92nd Cong., 1st Sess., 1971.

U.S. Congress, Joint Committee on Atomic Energy. *Hearings on Development, Growth, and State of the Nuclear Industry.* 93rd Cong., 2nd Sess., 1974.

——————. *Hearings on Environmental Effects of Producing Electric Power.* 91st Cong., 2nd Sess., 1969.

——————. *Issues for Consideration–Review of National Breeder Reactor Program.* Joint Committee Print. Washington: U.S. Government Printing Office, 1975.

——————. *Nuclear Power Plant Siting and Licensing.* Washington: U.S. Government Printing Office, 1974.

U.S. Congress, Joint Committee on Internal Revenue Taxation. *Analysis of Energy Supply, Conservation, and Conversion, an Analysis of H.R. 6860.* 94th Cong., 1st Sess., 1975.

——————. *Energy Taxation: Alternative Conservation Taxes.* Joint Committee Print. 93rd Cong., 2nd Sess., 1974.

U.S. Congress, Joint Economic Committee. *Hearings on Economic Impact of Environmental Regulations.* 93rd Cong., 2nd Sess., 1974.

——————. *Hearings on Financial and Capital Needs.* 93rd Cong., 2nd Sess., 1974.

——————. *Hearings on Gas and Electric Rates.* 93rd Cong., 2nd Sess., 1974.

U.S. Congress, Senate, Committee on Commerce. *Hearings on Electrical Energy Conservation Act.* 93rd Cong., 2nd Sess., 1974.

——————. *Hearings on Energy and Environmental Objectives.* 93rd Cong., 2nd Sess., 1974.

U.S. Congress, Senate, Committee on Finance. *Hearings on Capital Requirements for Energy Independence*. 94th Cong., 1st Sess., 1975.

U.S. Congress, Senate, Committee on Finance. *Hearings on Growing Threat of a Domestic Financial Crisis*. 93rd Cong., 2nd Sess., 1974.

U.S. Congress, Senate, Committee on Government Operations. *Electric and Gas Utility Rate and Fuel Adjustment Clause Increases, 1974*. Committee Print. 94th Cong., 1st Sess., 1974.

——————. *Hearings on the Utilities Act of 1975*. Washington: U.S. Government Printing Office, 1975.

U.S. Congress, Senate, Committee on Interior and Insular Affairs. *Factors Affecting Coal Substitution for Other Fossil Fuels in Electric Power Production and Industrial Uses*. Committee Print. 94th Cong., 1st Sess., 1975.

——————. *Hearings on Problems of Electrical Production in the Southwest*. 92nd Cong., 1st Sess., 1971.

——————. *Electric Utility Policy Issues*. Committee Print. 93rd Cong., 2nd Sess., 1974.

——————. *Hearings on Coal Policy Issues*. 93rd Cong., 1st Sess., 1973.

——————. *Hearings on Financial Problems of Electric Utilities*. 93rd Cong., 2nd Sess., 1974.

——————. *Highlights of Energy Legislation in the 94th Congress, Through June 30, 1974*. Committee Print. 94th Cong., 1st Sess., 1975.

U.S. Congress, Senate, Committee on Interior and Insular Affairs, Subcommittee on Water and Power Resources. *Hearings on Bonneville Power Administration Financing*. 93rd Cong., 2nd Sess., 1974.

U.S. Congress, Senate, Committee on Public Works. *Hearings on Granting Financial Incentives to the Tennessee Valley Authority for Construction Costs of Environmental Facilities*. 93rd Cong., 2nd Sess., 1974.

DAVID L. SCOTT is Associate Professor of Accounting and Finance in the School of Business Administration at Valdosta State College, Valdosta, Georgia. He was formerly on the faculty at Florida Southern College, Lakeland, Florida.

Dr. Scott is the author of the book *Pollution in the Electric Power Industry: Its Control and Costs,* which was published in 1973. He has published several articles on the options market and the electric utility industry.

Professor Scott was born in Rushville, Indiana. He received a B.S. from Purdue University, an M.S. from Florida State University, and the Ph.D. from the University of Arkansas.

**RELATED TITLES**
Published by
Praeger Special Studies

THE DYNAMICS OF ELECTRICAL ENERGY SUPPLY
AND DEMAND: An Economic Analysis
R. K. Pachauri

INFLATION: Long-Term Problems
edited by Lowell C. Harriss

WAGE AND PRICE CONTROLS: The U.S. Experiment
edited by John Kraft
and Blaine Roberts

Soc
HD
9685
U5
537